THE BRIDGE TO BRAILLE

THE BRIDGE TO BRAILLE

READING AND SCHOOL SUCCESS FOR THE YOUNG BLIND CHILD

Carol Castellano **Dawn Kosman**

Illustrated by Lynne Cucco

National Organization of Parents of Blind Children

Baltimore

NATIONAL ORGANIZATION OF
PARENTS OF BLIND CHILDREN
1800 Johnson Street
Baltimore, MD 21230

© 1997 by the NATIONAL ORGANIZATION OF
PARENTS OF BLIND CHILDREN
All rights reserved

Printed in the United States of America

Library of Congress Cataloging-in-Publication Data
Castellano, Carol, 1951-
    The bridge to braille: reading and school success for the young blind child / Carol Castellano, Dawn Kosman; illustrated by Lynne Cucco.
      p. cm.
    Includes bibliographical references (p.).
    ISBN 1-885218-08-7 (pbk.)
    1. Braille. 2. Children, Blind–Education (Elementary)
3. Children, Blind–Education (Early childhood)
I. Kosman, Dawn, 1960-   . II. Title.
HV1672.C37   1997
371.911–dc21   97-18720
                                                           CIP

Designed by Barbara Castellana Stasiak,
Wavelength Communications

Reference is made in this book to the following trademarks:
Apple®, Braillemate™, Braille 'n Speak®, Dycem®, Elmer's GluColors™, Fun-Tak®, Hi Marks™, IBM®, Macintosh®, Twin Vision®, Unifix®, Velcro®, Wikki Stix™

To parents of blind children everywhere; every time one of our kids makes it, the world becomes a better place for all of our kids.

       C.C.

To Serena Cucco and to all the blind students I have taught and who, in turn, have taught me.

       D.K.

*You can be anyone,
do anything,
or go any place
by reading a book.*

KAREN MESSICK
Children's Librarian
NJ Library for the Blind and Handicapped

PREFACE

What do you believe about the education and development of blind children? Can blind children achieve at the same level as sighted children of the same age or grade? Can they learn the same skills and concepts? Do they need to? Are blind people limited in certain ways? What does the future hold for a blind person? Can blind children grow up to be fully functioning, independent adults?

These questions are important because the way we approach the education and development of blind children will depend on what we believe about blindness and what blind people can achieve. Sometimes sighted people believe that blind people must be quite helpless because we cannot imagine being able to function without eyesight. If I were to lose my eyesight tomorrow, I would be relatively helpless, but there would be something I could do

THE BRIDGE TO BRAILLE

about it–I could learn the skills of blindness. The skills and tools of blindness are the key to accomplishing tasks without eyesight. The skills and tools of blindness enable blind people to function competitively and with success.

Our job, as parents and educators, is to learn as much as we can about these skills and tools. If we are familiar and comfortable with them, we will be more apt to give our blind children the opportunities they need to learn and practice them. This book was written to be a practical, step-by-step guide for parents and teachers. It will introduce the skills, tools, and adaptations the blind child will use to achieve success in reading, in school, and in life!

Once we realize that blind children can have a normal life, we then realize that our expectations for their achievement and for their future should also be normal. If we believe that blind children can have a normal life, then our children can grow up believing that, too. We can enable our children to have confidence in themselves, to dream and hope, to have aspirations for the future. What a gift for us to give!

In the spirit of keeping doors open and looking toward the future, it seems fitting to begin this book with an essay which I wrote about my daughter when she was nine years old.

Preface

POSSIBILITIES

It took my daughter Serena a long time to decide just what she wanted to be when she grew up. Whereas my son was only four when he decided that he would be a dinosaur scientist, it wasn't until she was seven that Serena realized that her destiny in life was to be a folksinger. Happily she played the chords to her favorite song, "Michael, Row the Boat Ashore," on my guitar.

Then came the Presidential campaign of 1992. Serena was eight. She sat rapt before the television, listening intently to the speeches of both parties. After the summer's two political conventions, she realized that it wasn't a folksinger that she wanted to be after all. It was . . . a folksinging Senator. By late fall, having heard all three Presidential debates, Serena was going to be President.

Her barrage of questions about how she could learn to be President and conversations about what politicians do kept up for a long time. My husband and I were convinced that our daughter might indeed go into politics when she was older.

In the late spring of that year, Serena went out with her father to pick early snow peas from the garden. Coming inside with her basket of peas, she told me she was *very* interested in gardening. "That's wonderful," I replied. "You'll be a big help to Daddy."

THE BRIDGE TO BRAILLE

Overnight Serena's interest must really have taken root, because the next day she asked me if I thought the gardens at the White House were too big for the President to tend, since the President is such a busy person. "Yes," I replied. "I'm sure there's a staff of people who take care of the White House gardens." "Well then, I won't be a gardening President," she told me. "I'll just be a gardener."

The desire to be a gardener was still but a tender shoot when Serena took a piano lesson–just a few weeks after picking those peas–and realized it was a pianist she wanted to be! After that, a wild enthusiasm for sports convinced her that radio sports announcing was the career for her.

Serena is at such a wonderful stage of life! Interested in everything, trying everything out, she sees the world as her plum, ripe for the picking. She believes in herself, as we believe in her. And since what people believe largely determines what they do, it is crucial for parents of blind children–and other adults in the child's life–to have positive beliefs about blindness and what blind people can do.

If we are told (in a journal article or by a teacher of the blind, say) that blind children usually do not or cannot learn how to do a certain task, and if we come to believe that, chances are we will not give our child the experience or opportunity *anyone* would need in

Preface

order to do that task. And chances are the child won't learn to do it. Imagine, though, if we—and our blind children—were *never* told that they could not accomplish a certain thing. Imagine what the results might be if everyone believed that blind people could do anything they wanted to!

Well, I believe that and I think I have good reason for it. Each year my husband and I attend the National Convention of the National Federation of the Blind. There we have met, or have heard speak, a blind high school teacher, college professor, mathematician, NASA scientist, chemist, car body mechanic, industrial arts teacher, transmission mechanic, Foreign Service officer, engineer, high-performance engine builder, and a man who sailed solo in races from San Francisco to Hawaii. These blind men and women approach life's challenges with a sense of excitement and creativity, asking not *whether* they can accomplish the task but *how* they will do it. Meeting blind people from so many walks of life has enabled my husband and me to see firsthand that blindness does not have to stop people from achieving what they want to achieve. This belief guides the way we bring up our daughter.

Sometimes in the professional literature, I read the phrase "accepting the child's blindness." That concept of acceptance always causes me some concern; to different people, it can mean entirely opposite things. To some, "accepting the child's blindness" means accepting–or coming to believe–that because the child is blind, there will be limits to what the child can do, limits to what he or she can understand, limits to what he or she can learn. (These beliefs are often referred to as "being realistic.") It is easy to see what the effects of that kind of thinking will be.

When I consider the term "accepting the child's blindness," I think about accepting *that* the child is blind, realizing that blindness need not stop the child from achieving what he or she wishes, and allowing, indeed insisting, that the child learn the alternative techniques of blindness that will enable him or her to achieve the desired results!

Find a way, parents and teachers. Keep all the doors open. Nurture creativity. Glory in the exhilarating feeling of watching a child look toward the future and see only *possibilities*.

CAROL CASTELLANO

Acknowledgements

We would like to thank the many friends and colleagues who reviewed the manuscript and offered comments, suggestions, and encouragement. We are grateful to classroom teachers Debbie DeHaven and Bebe Facciani and Braille teacher Terry Cerutti, who gave assistance on the earliest drafts of the manuscript; to Donald Carugati and David De Notaris, who offered their enthusiasm and their talent with words; to Valerie Ryan, Roseann Weinstein, and Kim Grant, who brought to the task their personal experiences as parents of blind children; to Jane Bente and Lee Calligan for their expertise in the technicalities of Braille transcription; to David Andrews and Marianne Agner, who shared their knowledge of Braille technology.

We would also like to thank Ruby Ryles, Research Associate at the International Braille Research Center, and Braille teacher Barbara Shalit for their thoughtful reading of the manuscript and their help with thinking through complex issues. Thanks also to Dr. Fred Schroeder, who is currently the U.S. Commissioner of

Rehabilitation Services, for his valuable perspectives both as Executive Director of the New Mexico Commission for the Blind and as a daily user of Braille. We express special gratitude to Braille teacher and author Doris Willoughby, who offered to read several drafts of the manuscript and generously shared not only her ideas and expertise, but also her eagle eye at catching typos.

We express our appreciation to Barbara Cheadle, Editor of *Future Reflections*, Joe Ruffalo, President of the National Federation of the Blind of New Jersey, and the members of the National Federation of the Blind for their support of this project.

Warm thanks go to Mina Albanese, Ellen Rice, and Gay Wilentz for their friendship and encouragement. Heartfelt appreciation goes to our librarian friends, Karen Messick and Margaret Anzul, for their constant enthusiasm and support for our work. We especially thank our friend and colleague, Joe Cutter, a devoted professional who is always willing to discuss ideas and who inspires us with his dedication to the education of blind children. We express loving thanks to our families for their love, patience, printer-lugging, and support.

The publication of this book was made possible by a generous grant from the Belleville, New Jersey, Lions Club. Thank you, Belleville Lions!

Contents

Setting the Stage for Success 3
Normal Life Activities Develop Skills
Language Development
Getting Ready for Reading Success
Additional Literacy Activities

A Quick Braille Lesson 13
Braille Contractions
Braille Numbers
Braille Writing
Troubleshooting
Learning Braille along with Your Child
Setting Up at Home

Adapting Materials 23
Readiness Worksheets
Math Worksheets
Labeling with Braille
Flashcards

THE BRIDGE TO BRAILLE

Beginning Braille Reading 33
Reading Readiness
Approaches to Teaching Braille
The Mechanics of Braille Reading
Reading Technique

Braille Reading Skills for School 43
Reading Placement
Keeping Up with the Group
Keeping Up with New Contractions
Dictionary Skills
The First Grade Challenge

About Braille Books 53
Literary Format
Textbook Format
Page Turns
Line Spacing
Volumes
Illustrations
Plastic Pages
Transcription Issues

Writing in Braille 71
Using the Braillewriter
Using the Slate and Stylus

Contents

Braille Writing in the Classroom 81

Practicing the Letters
Whole Language Writing
Correcting and Editing
Workbook Pages
Marking Answers
Spelling and Spelling Tests
Taking Notes

Doing Math in Braille 93

Nemeth Code
Getting Started with Numbers
Math Readiness
Beginning Addition and Subtraction
What Do Math Examples Look Like in Braille?
Writing Horizontal Problems
Writing Vertical Problems
Long Division
Must My Child Write Out All That Math?
Nemeth Code Cheat Sheet

Independence in the Classroom 119

Desk Size and Placement
Arranging Materials and Equipment
Keeping Paperwork in Order
Laying the Groundwork for Independence

THE BRIDGE TO BRAILLE

Using Technology 127
An Overview of High-Tech Devices
Choosing High-Tech Equipment

Resources 139
Helpful Items
Helpful Books
Sources of Braille Books
Sources of Materials, Books, and Information

Appendices 159
"Literacy, Learning, and Louis Braille"
"Making Whole Language Work"
"A Parent's Guide to the Slate and Stylus"

SETTING THE STAGE FOR SUCCESS

Setting the Stage for Success

It's natural for parents to want to start their preschoolers on the road to reading and school success. Parents of blind children are no different! Many parents, however, feel unsure of themselves when it comes to preparing their *blind* child for these activities. Believe it or not, most of the same strategies that apply to sighted children apply to blind children, too.

All children, in order to achieve success in school, must develop certain basic skills. Body awareness, fine and gross motor skills (small muscle and large muscle control), tactile discrimination (the ability to tell things apart by touch), language skills, listening skills, auditory discrimination (the ability to tell sounds apart), the ability to follow simple directions, an understanding of concepts (up/down, top/bottom, etc.), spatial awareness, sequencing skills, an increasing attention span, self-help skills, and socialization skills are some of the important skills.

THE BRIDGE TO BRAILLE

NORMAL LIFE ACTIVITIES DEVELOP SKILLS

How can parents play an active role in helping their child acquire these skills? Fortunately, these skills can be developed through play and through normal life activities. As you play "horsey" with your child on the living room floor, body awareness is developing; as you and your child mix batter for chocolate chip cookies, fine motor skills and sequencing are practiced. Organize your child's play area. As you show your child how to keep track of belongings and encourage him/her to make choices, he/she will gain valuable school readiness experiences. Inviting a neighborhood child to come along with you to the park provides social experience. So relax and have fun with your child! Ideas for readiness activities can be found in the books listed in Resources, page 146.

LANGUAGE DEVELOPMENT

As you share experiences with your child, use plenty of *words* so that your child develops a vocabulary for objects, textures, smells, actions, feelings, etc. Tell your child the names of things and actions and also provide a variety of adjectives and adverbs to describe them. When all these words are matched with actual experiences the child is having, a *meaningful* vocabulary will develop. This means that when your child hears and uses these words, he/she will truly understand what they mean.

Setting the Stage for Success

Language development is a key to many important parts of a child's development—intellectual growth, social ability, even emotional development and behavior. By using words, you provide the "glue" that connects activities and events in your child's world and helps him/her begin to organize these experiences in his/her mind. Words make your child begin to *understand*. Words provide the *meaning* and begin to move your child from the concrete world of sensations (what he/she can touch, hear, smell, taste, or see) to the conceptual world of thought, ideas, imagination, and reasoning. Encourage your child to wonder *why*, *how*, and *what if*. Help your child make the connections.

GETTING READY FOR READING SUCCESS

You have probably heard that it is very important to *read to* children. Children who are read to regularly are more likely to be successful in school! Now, you might be wondering, would reading to my blind child from a print book be helpful, even if he/she does not see the words? The answer is yes, it certainly is! Your child can learn much about the world by listening to stories. In addition, there are many books that are available in both Braille and print. If you read from these, your child will be able to "read along" with you, just as a sighted child would. Initially the child is not really reading and it doesn't even matter

THE BRIDGE TO BRAILLE

if his/her fingers are on the right words or not. "Reading along" allows the child to experience the written word along with hearing the story. In this way, your child begins to realize that there is a connection between the words he/she is hearing and the symbols on the page. Sign your child up for Braille book clubs and for services from your state's Library for the Blind and Physically Handicapped right away! (Sources for print/Braille books are listed in Resources, page 151.)

What goes along with being read to and learning about the world through books? Life experiences! Life experiences not only provide opportunities to develop skills, but they also afford the child the opportunity to succeed academically. Children who are given the opportunity to *explore and experience* the world around them are more able to understand the ideas they come across in books. The child who has never played in a park, for example, might have a hard time comprehending a story about children playing on a swing and a slide, but the child who has had this experience will be better able to understand what happens in the story.

In addition to being able to understand the events in a story, a child who knows what happens in real life will also be able also to make realistic predictions about what might happen next in a story. (Teachers

Setting the Stage for Success

always ask this kind of question!) Being able to make predictions is important not only for reading success, but also because it is part of the development of logic and thinking skills. By exposing your child to many situations, you are actually preparing him/her to be successful—in reading and in life!

ADDITIONAL LITERACY ACTIVITIES

In addition to reading to your child and offering him/her a rich menu of life experiences, there are more ways in which you can help literacy—the ability to read and write—develop.

- Make sure your child is aware of all the times that *you* read and how much you use written material in your home and work life.
- Take trips to the library for books to read to your child; read the titles out loud and let your child help choose the books to take home; take advantage of the recorded books that are available, too; many have interesting sound effects that make the story even more fun for a young child.
- Have your child help choose books to order from Braille book publishers or from your state's Library for the Blind (see Resources, page 151, for sources of Braille books).
- At reading time, let your child choose which book you will read; sometimes a child will

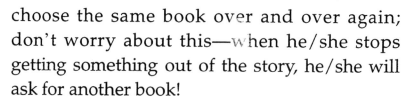

THE BRIDGE TO BRAILLE

choose the same book over and over again; don't worry about this—when he/she stops getting something out of the story, he/she will ask for another book!

- Before you begin reading, say the title of the book out loud and ask your child what he/she thinks the book might be about.
- Occasionally make comments about the story as you read and ask your child questions.
- Use real items that relate to the story as tactual "illustrations" for your child.
- After you finish reading, talk about the story; retell it together.
- Act out favorite stories; use sound effects and props!
- Make books about the child's everyday or special experiences—paste in real objects and a few lines of Braille; for example, *My Bathroom Book*—paste in a small bar of soap, a washcloth, a toothbrush and toothpaste, and a few sentences in Braille (see Learning Braille Along with Your Child, page 19).
- Let your child tell you a story; write the story down in Braille; read it back together.
- Have your child join you in writing activities—making out a shopping list, writing a thank you note, leaving a message for the babysitter.
- Encourage your child to play store, to pretend

Setting the Stage for Success

to pay bills, to play office, etc.; provide items to play with—an old telephone, an old checkbook register, index cards, a slate and stylus or Braillewriter—and let your child "scribble" away—in Braille, of course!

- Provide many opportunities for your child to "scribble," or pretend to write, on a Braillewriter or with a slate and stylus; scribbling in Braille could consist of simply making dots, to give the child the idea of writing.
- Adapt alphabet and counting toys and games by adding self-stick Braille labels (see Resources, page 143).
- Let your child try to copy letters or words you write in Braille.
- Help your child learn how to read and write his/her name in Braille.
- Try adapting other literacy activities for use with a blind child.

Remember, the purpose of these activities is to create an interest in and love of reading and writing. So be sure not to make any of these activities a chore!

A Quick Braille Lesson

A Quick Braille Lesson

Braille is simply another way of writing the alphabet. Braille reading and writing are the equivalent of print reading and writing. What the print reader reads and learns in print your Braille reader will read and learn in Braille.

The basic unit in Braille is called the Braille "cell." Each cell is made up of six dots, arranged in two columns of three dots each. The dots are numbered 1 to 6. Each Braille letter or other symbol is formed by using one or more of the six dots. (Small dots are often used to show empty dot positions.)

Sometimes cells are used in combination. For example, capitals are two-cell units formed by writing dot 6 (the capital sign) and then the letter.

THE BRIDGE TO BRAILLE

In actual Braille, the cells are always the same size. Beginning print readers learn from books that have very large letters, but beginning Braille readers learn to read using the same size Braille as advanced readers use.

First your child will learn the alphabet in Braille. Your child will not really be reading at this point, but will be learning to recognize the various letters. Sometimes Braille teachers do not teach the letters of the alphabet in order. This is because some of the letters that come near each other in the alphabet, such as *d, f, h,* and *j,* look similar in Braille and children can get confused. (The same is true for print letters *b, d, p,* and *q.*) The Braille teacher might introduce these letters out of alphabetical order and separate them by letters that look very different.

THE ALPHABET IN BRAILLE

a b c d e f g h i
j k l m n o p q r
s t u v w x y z

A Quick Braille Lesson

BRAILLE CONTRACTIONS

After your child learns the alphabet, he/she will begin to learn Braille contractions, as they come up in the reading material. Braille contractions are symbols made up of one or more cells that represent more than one letter. Braille uses contractions to save space. For example, the word *together* would be written *tgr* in contracted form. There are three categories of contractions—short-form, whole-word, and part-word. The contraction *tgr* is an example of a short-form contraction. The letter *c* when written alone stands for the word *can.* This is a whole-word contraction. The letters *d-i-s* are formed by just one cell in Braille and are an example of a part-word contraction.

A few Braille contractions

When Braille is written with no contractions, it is called *Grade 1 Braille.* Contracted Braille is called *Grade 2 Braille.* (The labels Grade 1 and Grade 2 refer only to uncontracted or contracted Braille and DO NOT in any way refer to first grade or second grade or any grade a blind child might be in!) The reading material that your child will see in books and worksheets will be written in Grade 2 (contracted) Braille. Children

The Bridge to Braille

use Grade 1 Braille only to learn the alphabet and perhaps later to take spelling tests or for phonics lessons. As soon as they begin to read, blind students use Grade 2 Braille.

Your child will learn the various rules of Braille usage and the Braille punctuation marks as he/she goes along. Punctuation marks are shaped like letters, but they are formed in the lower part of the cell, using only combinations of dots 2, 3, 5, and 6.

Braille Numbers

Learning numbers in Braille is simple—the first ten letters of the alphabet also serve as numbers, when written following a symbol called the number sign. For example, *a* is *1*, *b* is *2*, *c* is *3*, all the way up to *j*, which is *0*. Easy! When numbers are written this way they are called "literary" numbers. This is because they are formed from "literary Braille," the Braille your child will come across in books. The first numbers your child learns to read and write will probably be literary numbers.

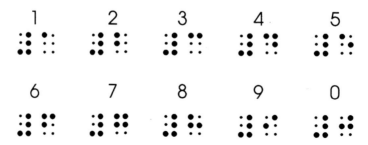

Literary numbers

A Quick Braille Lesson

When your child begins to learn math, he/she will be taught to read and write numbers in Nemeth Code, the name for math in Braille. In Nemeth Code, the shapes of the numbers are the same as their literary counterparts, but they are formed in the lower part of the cell, using only dots 2, 3, 5, and 6. The numbers your child will see in math books and worksheets will be Nemeth Code numbers. Your child will write his/her math using Nemeth numbers. (See Doing Math in Braille, page 93.)

Literary 2   Nemeth 2

         Literary 39   Nemeth 39

BRAILLE WRITING

Your child will probably initially be taught to write Braille on a Braillewriter. A Braillewriter is like a typewriter, but has only six keys. Each key forms a particular Braille dot. Combinations of the six keys form all the possible Braille symbols. Your child will also be taught to write Braille using a slate and stylus (see Writing in Braille, page 71).

THE BRIDGE TO BRAILLE

TROUBLESHOOTING

Sometimes a Braille teacher feels that a child who has learned the alphabet in Braille is not ready to learn contractions. If this occurs, it is still possible for the child to begin reading . Many simple words, such as all, ball, cat, hat, and sit, do not contain any contractions. Sentences for the child to read can be made using only words such as these. The following sentences contain no contractions: "My cat is furry" and "My dog is happy."

Sometimes Braille teachers use whole-word contractions to start the child reading. There are two kinds of whole-word contractions. The first kind consists of individual Braille letters which signify whole words when used alone—such as the letter *c*, which means *can* when used alone, as mentioned earlier, and the letter *d*, which means *do* when used alone. The second category of whole-word contraction consists of special symbols that signify words—for example, the word *for* is formed by pressing all six keys at one time to form a full six-dot cell. (The full cell also signifies the letters *f-o-r* in longer words like *forget* or *fort*.) Entire sentences can be formed using only whole-word contractions and other simple words, for example, "I do like you" and "You can have a can."

This method of teaching reading is popular because it gets children reading quickly, but make sure your child realizes that each of these symbols is

A Quick Braille Lesson

also a letter that has a sound and that these symbols usually appear next to other letters, to form words.

LEARNING BRAILLE ALONG WITH YOUR CHILD

Parents usually want to learn at least enough Braille to be able to check a child's work and help with homework. Many parents begin learning each Braille letter and contraction along with the child, beginning in preschool. If your child comes home from preschool with a "letter of the week" Brailled on a flashcard, you can memorize the shape of the letter in Braille, along with your child. Once you realize that Braille is simply another way to write the alphabet, you'll be on your way. Incidentally, most sighted people read Braille with their eyes. It's easy for parents to learn Braille because we, of course, have the advantage of already knowing how to read. We can also use a print "cheat sheet," which shows all the Braille letters and contractions on one page! (The book *Just Enough to Know Better,* discussed below, contains a cheat sheet.)

If you would like to learn enough Braille to stay one step ahead of your child, try *Just Enough to Know Better* (see Resources, page 146). You could also use a Braille-teaching textbook or take an online course. Your state's Library for the Blind, your child's Braille teacher, or a blind adult might also offer suggestions on how you can

THE BRIDGE TO BRAILLE

learn. The National Library Service for the Blind's booklet *Volunteers Who Produce Books* lists transcribing agencies that sponsor Braille transcribing classes.

SETTING UP AT HOME

Your child will have a Braillewriter in school and needs one at home, too, for homework and for other writing he/she might want to do—writing letters, taking down phone messages, making out a birthday party guest list, etc. The child can also use a slate and stylus for any of these tasks. You will also need a supply of Braille paper—both 8 ½" x 11" and 11 ½" x 11"—and large- and small-grid graph paper.

A complete set of all print textbooks and workbooks used in the classroom should be provided by the school for the home so you can easily get a sense of your child's homework and assist in the normal manner. Since the pages of Braille textbooks will be keyed to the print pages, it is easy to look something up in the print book.

After their child's homework is completed, many parents write in the print above each line of Braille for the benefit of classroom teachers, who will then be able to check the child's work right away and won't have to wait for the Braille teacher's visit. Transcribing the Braille into print also helps parents keep up their own Braille skills and keep track of the Braille signs the child is learning. (Later, blind students learn to type and can directly produce print papers for sighted teachers.)

ADAPTING MATERIALS

Adapting Materials

Readiness Worksheets

When your child enters a formal education program, whether it be preschool or kindergarten, chances are the classroom teacher will use some form of workbook or worksheets which introduce reading and math readiness skills in a structured way. For example, a worksheet might have rows of various shapes, letters, or numbers and children might be asked to circle the one that matches the first one on each line, or the one that is different. This should not be a cause for alarm. There are many ways to adapt such worksheets for a blind student. The classroom teacher, a teacher's aide, the Braille teacher, or the parent can prepare the materials.

Here are some ideas for adapting worksheets:

• Use pieces of different self-stick materials to represent the different shapes. Self-stick cork, plastic, felt, and Velcro, for example, have very different

textures that can easily be differentiated. These items are readily available in craft and discount stores.

• Cut shapes out of cardboard and attach them with glue or double-sided tape. Because of cardboard's heavier weight, cardboard shapes are easier to feel than shapes cut from plain paper. Little wooden shapes from a craft supplies store work well, too.

• Outline shapes with Hi Marks, T-shirt paints, or Elmer's GluColors (thicker than regular glue). Keep the outline simple; don't include a lot of detail. Use these materials well in advance to give the substance time to dry. GluColors dry faster than T-shirt paints and Hi Marks.

• Wikki Stix can be used to outline or create simple shapes. Wikki Stix is a craft/art item made of waxed string that can be bent into any position and can be stuck to and removed from paper. It is available at toy and craft stores.

• A tracing wheel from a sewing supplies store works for simple drawings, too. Place the worksheet wrong side up on a rubber pad or pile of newspapers. Trace over the lines *on the wrong side* of the paper and a bumpy raised line will appear on the right side of the paper for the child to feel.

• The Swail Dot Inverter and the Sewell Kit (items made specially for blind people—see Resources, page 142) can also be used for outlining shapes.

Adapting Materials

The key to adapting papers is to figure out what concept is being taught and then to decide how that concept can best be presented tactually. At times, the Braille page will not exactly match the print page because a different format will get the idea across better tactually. For example, the print page might have pictures spread around the page in a visually pleasing way. It might be best, though, to place the tactual items in a more structured way so that the blind child will be able to find them all.

MATH WORKSHEETS

Kindergarten and first grade math worksheets have many pictures with which the children learn to count, add, subtract, etc. Here are a few easy ideas for adapting such sheets when the teacher introduces the various concepts. Remember, although the pictures on the print page might be laid out for visual appeal, the tactual items should be placed in a structured way so that the blind child can locate and count them all.

• On the blind child's worksheet, the numbers can be Brailled and the pictures adapted with self-stick textures, GluColors, Wikki Stix, etc., as described above.

• Use full Braille cells to represent items pictured (press all keys at one time on the Braillewriter; leave a space after each full cell). Three ducks to count

THE BRIDGE TO BRAILLE

become three full cells to count. (The full cell is also called the *f-o-r* sign, as it is the way to write the word *for* or the letters *f-o-r* in Braille. It is commonly used in math books to represent pictures or blanks.)

• Another method is to use the first letter of what is pictured. For example, if the picture shows five bunnies and four porcupines, the blind child's paper can have five *b*'s and four *p*'s, with a space after each one.

• When the children are learning about coins and coin value, the numbers can be Brailled and actual pennies, nickels, and dimes can be examined. Do not attach the coins to the worksheet. Since blind people identify coins by their size and their smooth or ridged edges, the child needs to hold and examine the coins.

• If the sighted children are adding up coin value by using pictures of coins on their worksheets or paper coins, the blind child should use real coins. For the more advanced student, the paper can have the correct number of Brailled *p*'s to represent the number of pennies, a line of *n*'s for nickels, *d*'s for dimes, etc. The letters should be written with a space after each one.

LABELING WITH BRAILLE

Classroom teachers often prepare the way for children to begin reading by labeling various items

Adapting Materials

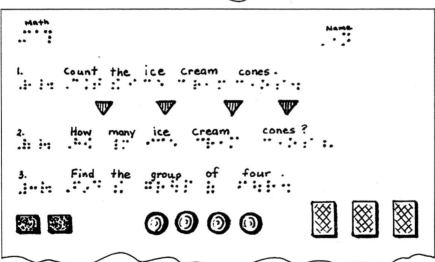

With adapted worksheets, the blind child is able to learn concepts along with the rest of the class

THE BRIDGE TO BRAILLE

around the room—desk, chair, cubby, etc. Teachers do not expect very young children to be able actually to read the words; the children are simply being exposed to the words. Teachers can easily make labels for a blind child by using a Braille labeler which makes instant Braille self-stick labels (see Resources, page 143). You can use a Braille labeler to label items at home, too.

FLASHCARDS

Teachers often make flashcards with students' names, color words, number words, etc., for use with the class. Cards like these can easily be made for the blind student by rolling an index card into the Braillewriter. Mark the top of each card so the child knows which way to hold it (a line of Braille *g*'s across the top will do the trick). Braille the word. Then write the word in print above the Braille word on each card. As the teacher holds up each print card for the class to view, he/she can hand the appropriate card to the blind student.

Blind children can also use flashcards to practice identifying capital and lower case letters, contractions, vocabulary "sight words," etc.

Adapting Materials

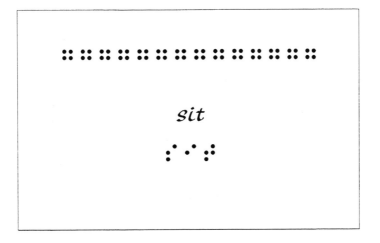

Flashcards are useful to practice beginning reading skills such as identifying capital and lower case letters and learning vocabulary sight words

BEGINNING BRAILLE READING

Beginning Braille Reading

Reading Readiness

Many skills lead up to actual reading, such as being able to locate the top and bottom of a page and the beginning and end of a line, and being able to tell the difference between shapes. Teachers refer to such skills as "reading readiness skills." Activities which help children gain these skills are called reading readiness activities.

Several programs are available that blind children can use to gain reading readiness (see Resources, page 147, for ordering information). *Tactual Discrimination Worksheets* provides excellent practice and can be used either along with a child's classroom program or on its own at home, if a child is not yet in school. This set provides an assortment of general reading readiness activities as well as tactile activities specific to Braille.

The Bridge to Braille

The *Mangold Developmental Program of Tactile Perception and Braille Letter Recognition* is designed to help children learn to recognize Braille letters and learn good reading technique—following lines smoothly, moving along the page speedily, etc. This program can also be used for a child to gain readiness skills.

When your child demonstrates motivation and adequate readiness skills, he/she can be considered ready to read.

Approaches to Teaching Braille

Many Braille teachers feel that at the beginning level, teaching Braille is teaching reading; at this point they are not separate entities. Since there are different approaches to teaching reading (and different approaches to teaching Braille), and since every child is an individual and should be treated as such, it would be impossible to recommend a blanket approach to Braille that would be suitable for every child. It is often best to employ several methods rather than strictly adhere to just one. Often the Braille teacher will coordinate Braille lessons with the classroom reading lesson in addition to using materials specific to teaching Braille.

Here are descriptions of a few Braille programs that can be quite useful with beginning readers (see Resources, page 148, for ordering information).

Beginning Braille Reading

Curriculum Guide for Braille Readiness

This guide provides activities, materials, and evaluation suggestions based on the following five approaches to teaching the Braille code:

- Approach A follows the classroom teacher's method of teaching reading to the class.
- Approach B is based on the whole-word method. The student is introduced to Braille words, contractions, and short-form words through experience stories, poems, songs, etc.
- Approach C follows the phonetic method of teaching.
- Approach D is based on the Braille code, its symbols, and their gross differences.
- Approach E is also based on the Braille code; it is aimed not at teaching reading, but at teaching the Braille composition and punctuation signs, dictionary signs, and special signs such as italics, brackets, etc.

In the *Curriculum Guide,* reference is made to the following materials (by the same author). They are extremely useful, whether used in conjunction with the *Curriculum Guide* or independently.

- *Discovering Braille: A Workbook for Beginning Readers*
- *Discovering Braille: A Workbook of Special Signs*
- *Learning to Read Braille Contractions*

THE BRIDGE TO BRAILLE

Patterns: The Primary Braille Reading Program

Patterns is a reading program which is actually based on Braille (instead of being a Brailled version of a print reading program). *Patterns* introduces Braille characters in a "controlled sequence," meaning in a particular order, beginning with what is easiest in Braille. (In Brailled versions of print reading programs, Braille signs are introduced to the student as they come up in the various stories, not necessarily in an order which is easy in Braille. This means that the child may need to learn many Braille contractions, including advanced ones, in a short period of time, if those words happen to be in the original print stories.)

Although it is designed to be a complete reading program for Braille users, *Patterns* is usually used as a supplement to the classroom reading curriculum. *Patterns* can also be a wonderful resource at the preschool level, if no other formal reading program has been introduced, and during the summer months, for reinforcement and extra Braille practice. *Patterns* goes from the readiness level to the third reader level. Textbooks and teacher's guides are provided in print and Braille. *Patterns'* "library series," books intended for leisure reading, are provided in Braille only. (For a detailed plan for using *Patterns*, see *Handbook for Itinerant and Resources Teachers of Blind and Visually Impaired Students*, listed in Resources, page 148.)

Beginning Braille Reading

Mangold Developmental Program of Tactile Perception and Braille Letter Recognition

This program, as mentioned in the Reading Readiness section, is designed with two goals in mind: to help students master the recognition of Braille letters and to increase reading speed. The program can also be used for remedial work. The set includes practice worksheets, games, enrichment activities, and daily one-minute timings. A corkboard and pushpins that can be used with the worksheets are also included. (Tack the worksheets onto the corkboard; have the child mark each answer with a pushpin.) Children usually find it fun to work with these items, which are good for fine motor development, too.

Experience Stories

Many classroom teachers, especially those using the whole language approach to teaching reading, use experience stories as one component of their reading program. Experience stories are also used by Braille teachers to introduce Braille reading or to supplement the classroom reading program.

To create an experience story, the child relates an experience to the teacher, who writes down what the child says (the blind child's words would be transcribed into Braille, of course). For example, "I went to Aunt Ellen's house. There was a big dog. I jumped

THE BRIDGE TO BRAILLE

when the dog barked." Then together, teacher and student move their fingers across the Braille lines and "read" the story out loud. The child will not really be reading at first, but will soon begin to relate the symbols on the paper to the words being spoken, an important step in learning to read.

THE MECHANICS OF BRAILLE READING

In order for your child to read speedily and comfortably, set the book on a flat surface not higher than elbow level. The bottom edge of the book should be parallel with the child's shoulders. The child's arms should rest at a comfortable angle.

In order for the fingertips to touch the Braille properly, the fingers should be rounded. The Braille cell is sized to be easily covered by the fingertip pads, the area which actually perceives the dots in order to read. To practice correct rounded finger position, the child can line up all of his/her fingertips along the groove in a ruler or in the binding of a hardcover book and slide them from side to side.

Fingers do not perceive Braille by just touching or resting on the dots; movement across the dots is necessary. Very light touch should be used. Heavier pressure actually decreases perception. Interestingly, extremely good touch sensitivity is not necessary for Braille reading; so take heart, even if your child has a condition that diminishes his/her sense of touch.

Beginning Braille Reading

Braille readers recognize Braille characters by their total shape, not by their individual dots, so encourage your Braille reader to move his/her hands smoothly and lightly across the letters or words, without stopping unnecessarily on each letter. Discourage extra movements such as backtracking and "scrubbing," which is stopping on a Braille cell and repeatedly moving the finger up and down. These practices will produce much slower reading!

Children should be encouraged to use two hands to read, as this almost always allows for speedier, smoother reading, and to keep as many fingers as possible on a line of Braille. Tell your child, "Lots of fingers on the Braille."

Troubleshooting

Believe it or not, it is possible for a blind child to learn to write in Braille without being able to read at all! This can happen if the child is taught to concentrate only on dot numbers and pressing keys. To learn to *read* Braille, the child must have experience moving the fingers across the letters or words. Remember, Braille writing is by dot number; Braille reading is by shape. So make sure your beginning Braille reader develops the habit of reading what he/she has written after completing each line.

THE BRIDGE TO BRAILLE

READING TECHNIQUE

Here is a technique that usually works well for beginning readers. This method helps new readers keep their place. Keep index fingers next to each other and touching throughout the following movements:

    Hands together at the left
    Read across the line to the right
    Go back across the line to the beginning at the left
    Move down to the next line
    Repeat

After a child has become more proficient in moving across the Braille lines, he/she may develop an individual technique. Make sure the technique is providing for efficient reading. The speediest Braille readers use the following technique:

    Hands together at the left
    Move across the line toward the right
    Midway across, the left hand drops down and
        begins to read the next line while the right
        hand finishes reading the previous line
    Right hand joins left hand on the next line
    Continue

BRAILLE READING SKILLS FOR SCHOOL

Braille Reading Skills for School

Reading Placement

If your child's school groups children by reading ability or decides on reading material based on reading ability, you might have to take extra care to ensure that your blind child is placed appropriately. Classroom teachers consider many things when deciding on reading placement, such as the child's comprehension of written material, ability to decode words, understanding of vocabulary, reading speed, general working speed, etc. Unfortunately, it does sometimes happen that teachers make judgments about a blind child's ability and potential based not on the child's actual ability but on misunderstandings about blindness and Braille. For example, a teacher may not be quite able to believe that blind people are able to learn efficiently or that taking in information through the fingers is equivalent to taking in information through the eyes. Or he/she might have heard

The Bridge to Braille

that "Braille is slow." (A demonstration of reading by a blind adult can be useful to dispel this belief.) A teacher might assume that because of blindness the child will not be able to understand what is read.

Good teamwork and open communication among parents, Braille teacher, and school will help to ensure that the child is placed properly. The parents can provide information about the child's experiences and understanding; the Braille teacher can report on progress in decoding and other reading skills; the teacher can explain his/her criteria for the various placements.

Deciding on the appropriate reading placement might have to be done earlier than usual for a blind student because the books usually have to be sent out in advance to be Brailled. This means that there may not be the flexibility to change groups or levels that the sighted students enjoy. A print reader who is in the wrong group can simply be moved and handed the other reading book. A blind student would have to wait for the new reading materials to be Brailled. It is therefore very important that the person deciding on the blind child's placement have all the information he/she needs to make a good decision. Incidentally, if your child's school uses the whole language approach in which the entire class is reading the same book, the reading placement issue will probably not arise. (See "Making Whole Language Work," page 163, for details

on how a Braille reader can participate fully in a whole language program.)

KEEPING UP WITH THE GROUP

As do their sighted friends, blind children need to learn many classroom reading skills in Kindergarten and first grade. These skills include finding the page quickly, page turns, keeping the place, following along when others read aloud, keeping up with the reading pace, and moving fingers smoothly across the Braille page.

If your child is having difficulty keeping up with the pace during reading time, a teacher or teacher's aide could assist, but keep in mind that the ultimate goal is for the child to be able to handle these tasks unassisted.

Here are some ideas for helping your child learn to keep up independently:

- Practice two-handed reading with "lots of fingers on the Braille."
- Read aloud while your child follows along in the Braille book; then stop and see if the child is at the right place; take turns reading aloud; vary your reading speed.
- Have the child practice reading at a fast pace by using familiar or very simple material.

The Bridge to Braille

- Discourage your child from mouthing the words while reading silently; mouthing the words will slow him/her down.
- Teach skimming—moving the fingers lightly over the words to catch important sections, such as key words or the beginnings and ends of sentences; this is helpful for keeping up while someone else reads aloud.
- Practice finding the page quickly.
- Practice fast page turns and finding the first line of Braille on the new page.
- Let the classroom teacher know that the Braille page turns may not match the print page turns (see About Braille Books, page 53).
- Ask an adult blind friend to demonstrate good reading technique to the child.
- HAVE YOUR CHILD READ EVERY DAY!!!—fifteen minutes or so in first grade, twenty to thirty in second and third.

KEEPING UP WITH NEW CONTRACTIONS

The books your child will be learning from in reading class were probably transcribed into Braille from print originals. Beginner-level print reading books contain words which are easy to learn in print but are not necessarily easy to learn in Braille! This means that your child might be learning several

Braille Reading Skills for School

new contractions each day, as the various words come up in the reading book. You might want to keep track of the contractions your child is expected to know by marking them on a print "cheat sheet." Then you can give your child practice with those contractions at home.

Occasionally during reading class, a blind student will come across a contraction that has not yet been introduced by the Braille teacher. When this occurs, the classroom teacher can look up the contraction on a "cheat sheet" or in a contraction dictionary, or the child can mark it with a snip of Wikki Stix for the Braille teacher to teach or reinforce later. Pre-cut pieces of Wikki Stix should be kept in a place where the child can find and use them independently (see Independence in the Classroom, page 119).

DICTIONARY SKILLS

An important skill your Braille reader will be learning in school is how to use the dictionary. Because a Braille dictionary is quite large and contains many volumes, it might be appropriate to modify classroom dictionary lessons. For example, if the teacher assigns a list of words for the children to look up, he/she could give the blind child words that would all be found in one volume. Another idea is for someone to assist a young child in locating the correct volume.

THE BRIDGE TO BRAILLE

Talking electronic dictionaries exist and are quite useful for some tasks. But for understanding page formats, looking for words in alphabetical order, using guide words, using the pronunciation key, and learning other dictionary skills that your child certainly needs to know, your child will need to have his/her hands on a Braille book!

THE FIRST GRADE CHALLENGE

Readers who have mastered the Braille code read with the same competence, assurance, speed, and pleasure as their print-reading counterparts. The first year of Braille reading, however, could be considered more challenging than the first year of print reading, since the blind child is expected to master some sophisticated material at an earlier stage than print-reading classmates. For example, a Braille period is shaped like a *d* but appears in a lower position. Your beginning reader might read the word *fun* at the end of a sentence as *fund*, mistaking the period for a *d*. The beginning Braille reader must learn to differentiate these sometimes subtle differences.

The Braille period is shaped like a *d* but appears in a lower position in the cell

Braille Reading Skills for School

Another issue that might surface in first grade has to do with "reversals." Classroom teachers are thoroughly familiar with letters that are commonly confused in print, such as *b* and *d*. They are usually *not* familiar with those that occur in Braille, such as *m* and *sh*. You might need to alert the classroom teacher to these characteristics of Braille so that he/she does not think your child doesn't know the letter sounds! If you are aware of these challenges, you can support your new reader as he/she gains experience and competence.

made   shade

You will soon see that Braille is a wonderful, useful, usable system that allows full literacy for blind people and which children usually master with enjoyment and pride. In those areas where it seems a little more complicated than print, we adults can respect what the child has accomplished and appreciate the adaptability of humans. To the child, it is simply learning to read!

ABOUT BRAILLE BOOKS

About Braille Books

Many of the books that are published in print are also available in Braille, with more becoming available each year. Advances in computer technology have made it possible for Braille books to be stored on disk and then produced on Braille embossers as needed, so that today blind children and adults have access to many more Braille books than they did in the past.

Certain books are chosen to be transcribed into Braille by the National Library Service for the Blind and Physically Handicapped. These books can then be acquired by libraries for the blind across the nation. Other books are transcribed by volunteers in transcribing agencies in the various states. Still others are produced by Braille book publishers and are available for purchase. Braille books are mailed free of charge to blind people. For sources of Braille books, see Resources, page 151.

The Bridge to Braille

Almost all of the books available in Braille have been transcribed into Braille from a print original. Although the words contained in the two versions will be exactly the same, the Braille version of the book will usually have more pages than the print version. This is because one print page usually translates into more than one Braille page.

Books transcribed for pleasure reading are done in "literary format." When transcribers are Brailling books for classroom use, they use what is called "textbook format." An important difference between the two formats is how the pages are numbered.

Literary Format

The books your child reads for pleasure, such as those he/she receives from the state or regional Library for the Blind or from Braille book publishers, will be transcribed in literary format. When books are transcribed in literary format, the Braille version of the book usually has more pages than the print version. The Braille pages are numbered consecutively and the page numbers in the Braille book *do not match* the page numbers in the print original. The page numbers appear in the upper right corner of each Braille page.

In beginner pleasure books, when there are only a few words on each print page, a Braille transcriber

About Braille Books

might transcribe "page for page" or might transcribe *more* than one print page onto a single Braille page.

TEXTBOOK FORMAT

In textbook format, the Braille pages *are keyed to* the print pages. This is done so that when the classroom teacher tells the class to turn to a certain page, the blind student can turn to that page along with everyone else.

One print page usually translates into more than one Braille page; therefore, several Braille pages might be keyed to that one print page. Here is an example of how this works. If print page 36 takes up three Braille pages, those Braille pages will be numbered 36, a36, b36. Print page 37 might become Braille pages 37, a37, b37, c37. These page numbers will appear in the upper right corner of the page. (The consecutive Braille page numbers are placed in the lower right corner.) To follow along in class, the blind student would look at the page numbers in the upper right.

When transcribers begin transcribing a new print page, they will continue on the previous Braille page, if there is still room. This means, for example, that print page 38 may begin on the same sheet as Braille page c37. When this occurs, the words from the new print page will be separated from those of the previous

THE BRIDGE TO BRAILLE

print page by a line of Braille dots. The new print page number will appear in Braille at the end of the dotted line.

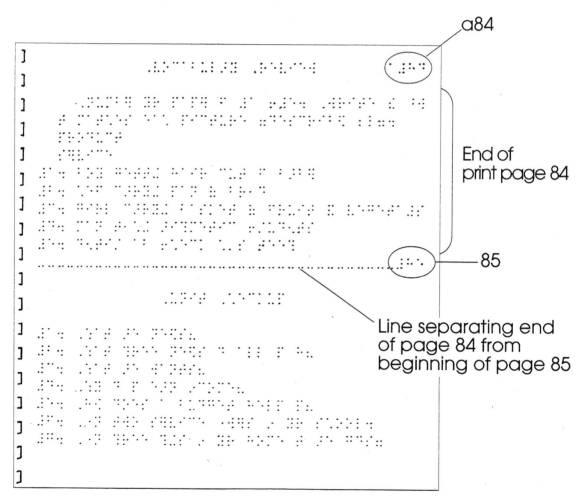

A page of a book transcribed in textbook format

About Braille Books

Troubleshooting

If a fiction book is going to be used as a classroom text (for example, in a whole language classroom), it will either be sent out to a transcriber to be Brailled or be ordered from the Library for the Blind or a Braille book publisher. If sent to a transcriber, the book will be transcribed in textbook format, and the page numbers in the Braille book will be keyed to those in the print book. However, if the book has been ordered from the Library for the Blind or from a Braille book publisher, then it will *not* be in textbook format *and the page numbers will not match.* When this occurs, make sure the teacher knows, so that if pages are assigned, the Braille student has a way of finding the assigned section in his/her book. For example, the teacher might assign pages 95 to 100 for the students to read, but in the Braille book, this same section might appear on pages 145 to 155. The blind student needs a chapter number, first words in a paragraph, or some other way to locate the assigned section.

Page Turns

As you have seen, page numbers in the Braille book may or may not match page numbers in the print book and page *turns* almost certainly will not match. You will quickly notice this if you are reading along in print while your child is reading in Braille.

THE BRIDGE TO BRAILLE

This is usually not a problem, but when it occurs in reading group in first grade, it is helpful for the classroom teacher to be aware of it, especially while children are first learning to follow along and are supposed to be on the same page as everyone else! It is also helpful for the teacher to understand that when he/she tells the children to look at the sentence at the bottom of page 14, that sentence might appear at the top of page b14 for your Braille reader! Some Braille transcribing agencies make it a point to transcribe first grade reading books "page for page," but others do not. Alert the teacher to such differences and at the same time, begin teaching your child how to interpret instructions meant for the print users in the classroom.

LINE SPACING

As you become accustomed to looking at the pages of Braille books, you will notice that Braille books at the beginner level are double spaced. Single-spaced lines begin to appear at the second reader level. When your child switches from double- to single-spaced books, give him/her sufficient practice in order to get used to the new spacing.

As your Braille reader advances in reading skill, the day will come when he/she is reading single-spaced, double-sided all-Braille books! Since it is

About Braille Books

difficult to read the Braille in such books visually, it is helpful to have a print copy of the book available at home. This way, you or other family members can enjoy following along when the child reads aloud and offer ordinary help if the child gets stuck on a word.

VOLUMES

In longer books, the Braille pages will be separated into volumes. On the first pages of each volume, a note in print and Braille tells how many volumes there are in all, the volume number, and which print and Braille pages are contained in that volume. A math textbook volume, for example, might say, "A-W Math 4, in 18 Volumes, Volume 1, Braille Pages p1-p3 and 1-57, Print Pages 1-54."

The blind child will need the current volume of the book handy at his/her desk in school and will also need to bring home the correct volume or volumes of the book in order to complete homework assignments. Make sure your child learns to pay attention to the page numbers of the volumes so that he/she will know when it is time to get the next one and won't have to spend class time looking for volumes. The note identifying each volume and its pages is placed at the bottom of the first Braille page so that if the books are standing in a book shelf, the student can simply reach under the cover, read

which pages are included in that volume, and grab the needed volume.

Some textbooks have glossaries, appendices, or supplements at the end of the book, which teachers might use for class and homework assignments. These will be in the last volumes of the Braille version of the book. Make sure your child is able to locate these volumes when work in those pages is assigned.

Illustrations

Primary Level Books

Primary level pleasure books contain many pictures and, in fact, are often referred to as "picture books." In general, pictures do not appear in the Braille version of these books. Sometimes, however, Braille descriptions of the illustrations are included. When these appear, they are separated from the words of the story by "boxing lines," which look like a line of Braille *g*'s across the page above and below the description.

Often in children's picture books, the characters are animals—raccoons or bunnies or bears which are acting like humans. This information is often transmitted through the pictures. Make sure your blind child gets this information.

Typical primary level textbooks also contain many illustrations. Some illustrations are included

About Braille Books

for beauty or entertainment and some contain important information that the children will use. The Braille versions of these textbooks, however, almost never contain the pictures. Therefore, the blind student does not get the information that the sighted students get from the illustrations. Make sure your child's teacher is aware of this.

In order to give the blind child access to the information, the teacher can describe the pictures or can have the class discuss them. This would be important if the pictures help carry the plot in a story, or give information or clues for understanding the story or answering questions.

Math Textbooks

Primary level math books contain many pictures for counting, adding, and subtracting. The Braille version of these books may have simple figures such as squares or circles to take the place of the print pictures, or may have the first letter of the item pictured. For example, if the print page shows five bunnies, the Braille page might have five *b*'s. Braille *x*'s or full cells (*f-o-r* signs) might also be used.

Math textbooks contain many kinds of illustrations which are used to teach concepts. In general, these figures are included in the Braille version of the books. The exception to this is 3-dimensional figures,

The Bridge to Braille

which may or may not be included. It is often more useful for the blind student to examine a real object rather than to try to learn this kind of concept from a raised-line drawing. For example, if the class is learning about cubes, the blind student can examine a cardboard box.

Phonics Books

Sometimes a textbook will not be Brailled at all, if the print book is too dependent on pictures. Unfortunately, this can happen with first and second grade phonics books.

If the blind student has no Brailled phonics book, he/she might not get the same practice in phonics skills as sighted classmates. In order to ensure that the blind student gets phonics practice, teachers will need to analyze the skills being taught and then adapt the various pages of the print phonics book. One possibility is for the Braille teacher to transcribe the *written* parts of the pages into Braille for the child to examine while someone says the name of each item pictured to the child. The child can then Braille or dictate the answers.

The important thing to remember is that the blind child needs the same opportunities to learn and practice these skills as his/her sighted classmates.

About Braille Books

Phonics   Name _____

Write the beginning sound.

First and second grade phonics books are often too dependent on pictures to be Brailled

THE BRIDGE TO BRAILLE

Social Studies and Science

In social studies and science texts, the captions that appear below drawings and photographs will be Brailled, but the illustrations themselves will probably be omitted. In general, maps are omitted from social studies texts. Blind students have access to raised-line maps from the American Printing House for the Blind and other sources. They can learn map skills from these raised-line maps, although they will not be working with the same maps that their classmates are using. Another alternative is for teachers to enlarge and then adapt print maps with Wikki Stix, self-stick textures, drafting tape, etc. Relief maps are also available from map stores.

PLASTIC PAGES

Before the age of computer Braille transcription (which began in the mid-eighties), the Braille version of textbooks and workbooks were reproduced on plastic sheets. Nowadays, almost all Braille textbooks are produced by computer on paper sheets, except for pages containing raised-line drawings, which are still produced on plastic sheets. It is possible, however, that your child will come across all-plastic books.

Although plastic pages present no difficulty for more advanced Braille readers, plastic is not the best

About Braille Books

surface for beginning Braille readers to read from. Fingers can stick to a plastic surface, which interferes with fluid hand and finger movement. Also, the plastic pages can slip and slide on the desk as the child attempts to move his/her fingers across the Braille lines. In addition, the dots produced on plastic pages are not crisp and sharp.

Beginning readers deserve high quality, crisp Braille, but you may find that some of your child's first and second grade books were indeed produced on plastic sheets. If your young child must read from plastic pages, a rubber pad or sheet of Dycem (see Resources, page 143) inserted under the book page will reduce slippage. (A rubber pad or Dycem sheet also keeps other kinds of Braille paper, flashcards, playing cards, etc. from sliding around on smooth surfaces.)

TRANSCRIPTION ISSUES
Mistakes in the Braille

Most of what your Braille reader will be working on in school will be just the same as what his/her sighted classmates are doing. There is an area of difficulty, however, that a Braille user might encounter that print readers will not. In the Braille versions of textbooks, mistakes are sometimes made in the transcription—addition signs instead of subtraction,

The Bridge to Braille

incorrect numbers or letters, etc.—that are not caught during proofreading. (Sometimes delays in getting print books to the transcribers are a cause of this problem; the transcribers need adequate time to Braille and proofread each book.) Advances in computer proofreading programs are helping to alleviate this situation, but it does still exist. Before you assume the child has made a mistake in reading or in copying an example, check the Braille against the print.

Page Format

Another transcription issue involves the format of the information given on the page. Although the transcriber has discretion, within certain guidelines, to decide how to arrange the information on the page, the transcriber's main charge is to create an accurate copy in Braille of the print page. In the past, this was not a problem, because the material on the print page was presented in a straightforward manner. Many of today's textbooks, however, are designed for visual excitement. A transcriber might follow the format of the print page and produce an accurate Braille copy of the print page, but the format may not work as well tactually as it does visually.

This problem is especially apparent in math books. When it occurs, the information on the Braille

About Braille Books

page will not be as easily accessible to the blind student as the information on the print page is to the sighted student. If you find this problem in your child's textbooks, check the print page and translate the information into a more accessible form for your child. This issue is generally more of a problem for young beginners than for more experienced Braille readers.

Another format issue is that sometimes there is not the same consistency among lessons or chapters in the Braille book that is found in the print version of a book. This lack of consistency can occur because the transcriber has discretion to decide how to format each page or lesson or because one book might be divided among several transcribers. Transcribing agencies vary in their policies about sending sections of the same book out to more than one transcriber. Sometimes this occurs because the transcribing agency was not given adequate time to Braille the book.

A lack of consistency among chapters or lessons is most problematic when it occurs in math books. In addition to learning how to do the actual math, the young Braille user may have to spend time interpreting page formats. Again, although this causes little difficulty for older students, it can be confusing for young beginners.

THE BRIDGE TO BRAILLE

Omissions

Another troublesome issue is that certain material which is too visual to be transcribed into Braille is omitted–this might be illustrations, photographs, maps, diagrams, etc. Questions on the page may refer to visual material that has been omitted. Sometimes there is a sentence alerting the student to the omission and sometimes there is not! Again, more experienced Braille readers become accustomed to this situation, but beginners may need help in understanding the page or in recognizing when to get help from the teacher.

If the Braille book has omissions, then the blind student may be missing important information. When this occurs, teachers must devise alternate means to ensure that the blind student gets the information.

Be sure that classroom teachers understand these format issues, so that your child gets equal access to information and is not unfairly penalized.

WRITING IN BRAILLE

WRITING IN BRAILLE

USING THE BRAILLEWRITER

Braille writing is taught, for the most part, hand in hand with reading. Most blind children initially learn to write on a Braillewriter. Once a child is able to follow simple directions, identify the right and left hands, and press down on the keys of the Braillewriter, he/she can begin writing.

The Braillewriter has six keys, each of which corresponds to a dot in the Braille cell. Pressing a key on the Braillewriter will produce a dot. Pressing two keys at the same time will produce two dots. For example, the letter *a* in Braille is dot 1. To write an *a*, press key 1. To write letter *b* (dots 1, 2), press keys 1 and 2 at the same time. To write a capital *a*, press key 6 (for dot 6, the capital sign), let the key up, and then press key 1 (for dot 1, the *a*). Capital *b* would be key 6, let up, then keys 1 and 2 together. Your child's Braille teacher will probably teach writing the letters by dot

THE BRIDGE TO BRAILLE

number. Parents sometimes number the Braillewriter keys for themselves while they are learning (use small pieces of masking tape and waterproof marker).

Soon after your child has learned even just a few letters, he/she will be able to write simple words. For example, *all, ball,* and *call* can all be written after just four letters have been learned. Have your child read what he/she has written on each line. Remember, Braille writing is by dot number, but Braille reading is not. Braille readers recognize the characters by their total shape, so teach your child to move the hands smoothly and lightly across the words.

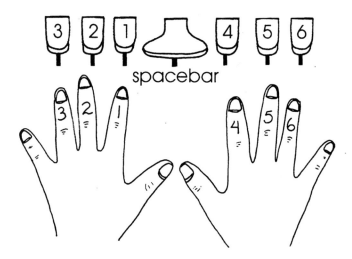

The Braille teacher will teach your child correct fingering for the Braillewriter. The index, middle, and ring fingers of each hand are used to press the keys. The thumb is used for the spacebar.

Writing in Braille

It might take some time for a young child to learn to press the keys of the Braillewriter with adequate pressure, so be sure your child has ample opportunity to practice. Your preschooler can get this practice as he/she "scribbles" on the Braillewriter. If your child has severe muscle weakness that makes it extremely difficult to press the keys, he/she can use an electric Braillewriter or key extenders on a manual Braillewriter to make pressing the keys easier. Adaptive items such as key extenders are useful when they are truly needed, but if your child can use the regular, unadapted item, then he/she should!

Inserting the Paper

Learning to insert paper into the Braillewriter independently is usually an early goal for the blind child. The following story can help young students get started. (The source of this story is unknown.)

> Tommy Turtle (embossing head) is very hungry. If you feed him some paper, he will help you write your letters. First you must always check to see if his paper feed knobs are in the right position, away from you (demonstrate by turning knobs away from you as far as they will go). Now let's be sure Tommy Turtle is where he belongs before we open his cage. Grab

The Bridge to Braille

hold of his leash (embossing head lever) and pull him all the way over to the left. (Demonstrate that moving the embossing head lever also moves the embossing head.)

Now let's make sure Tommy's cage door is open (demonstrate pulling the paper release/lock lever toward you). We're almost ready to put the food on his plate, but first we have to make sure the holes of the paper are on the left side. That's where Tommy Turtle likes them.

Here comes the tough part. Tommy Turtle is very fussy. He likes his food put on his plate very carefully. Start by feeding him the bottom left hand corner of the paper. Gently put it down on his plate (stripper plate). Try to keep the paper nice and straight. Now push the whole piece in under the roller. Then slide it to the left, as far as it will go.

Tommy Turtle is almost ready to gobble up his food, but you must be sure to lock his cage first (demonstrate how to push the paper release/lock lever away from you). Now take hold of the paper feed knobs, turn them toward you all the way, and watch Tommy Turtle gobble up the paper!

Writing in Braille

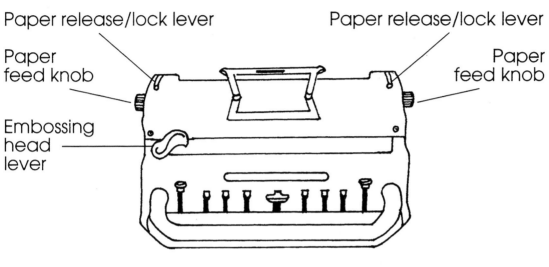

The Braillewriter

Children often need a good deal of practice before they can complete this task unassisted. As they become more adept at using the Braillewriter, they also learn how to set the margins themselves.

USING THE SLATE AND STYLUS

Your blind child will also learn how to write using a slate and stylus. The slate and stylus is the most portable of all Braille writing devices. It is often referred to as "the Braille user's paper and pencil." Many teachers introduce the slate and stylus in third grade, when sighted children begin to learn cursive writing. This can be the natural time for the blind student to work on another method of writing, too.

The Bridge to Braille

The slate is a folding metal or plastic frame, rectangular in shape, and hinged at the left side. The slate holds the paper. The top layer of the slate has rows of empty cells with six notches around the edge of each cell. The notches correspond to the six dots of Braille. The bottom layer of the slate has shallow depressions below each cell. The paper is placed between the two layers of the slate.

The stylus is the writing instrument; it consists of a metal point held in a wooden or plastic handle. Dots are formed by pressing the stylus against the notches and into the depressions of the slate. Writing on the slate begins at the right edge of the paper. Turn the paper over to read the Braille. (For more details on writing with a slate and stylus, see "A Parent's Guide to the Slate and Stylus," page 171.)

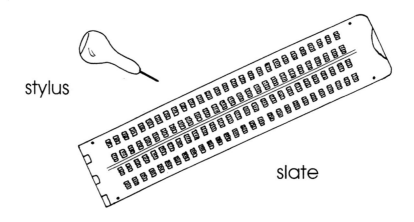

stylus

slate

Writing in Braille

You might hear that the slate and stylus is difficult to learn or that it has been made obsolete by modern technology. But children usually enjoy learning it and it really should be thought of as an additional–and very useful–tool that blind people can have at their disposal. Blind adults use it as a quick and efficient way to write out a shopping list, keep a check register, make notations on print notices, take notes at a meeting, and for countless other tasks. Many blind people keep a slate and stylus next to every phone in the house in order to jot down messages. Blind college students often prefer the slate and stylus for taking notes in their lecture classes. In addition, the slate and stylus has advantages that no other writing device for blind people has—it is small, light, quiet, portable, and inexpensive. It doesn't require batteries or an outlet and it is the only portable Braille writing device that uses paper.

BRAILLE WRITING IN THE CLASSROOM

Braille Writing in the Classroom

When a child enters preschool or kindergarten he/she will probably begin to write the letters of the alphabet and the numbers from 1 to 20. A blind child learns and practices writing in the same way as a sighted child, but uses a Braillewriter instead of a pencil.

Practicing the Letters

When the teacher introduces the letters to the class, the blind student should write them, too. Remember, Braille is the equivalent of print! If the sighted students are writing a row of each letter, the blind child should also write rows of letters. When

THE BRIDGE TO BRAILLE

writing rows of letters, the blind student should leave a space after each letter (by pressing the space bar after each letter) and double line space between rows (by pressing the line space lever twice after each row).

Activities in which students discriminate between or match capitals and lower case letters are appropriate for the blind student, as well. In general, all activities categorized as "visual discrimination activities" for sighted students will be relevant for the blind student, too. The blind student will simply do these tasks tactually.

Self-stick Braille alphabet and number lines can be placed at the edge of the child's desk as references while the child is learning to read and write. Sighted children are able to refer to alphabet and number cards mounted over the blackboard or around the room; it can be helpful for the blind child to have such references, too.

Beginning Braille users, like beginning print users, are taught to double line space. This makes it easier to read what has been written. It can be a good idea for your child to double line space until single spacing is introduced in books (second grade level) or until the child demonstrates the ability to read single-spaced Braille. Children can continue to double line space when working on writing projects, as it allows for easier editing and revising of drafts.

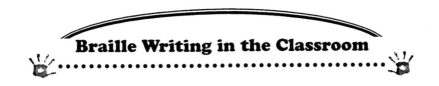

Braille Writing in the Classroom

WHOLE LANGUAGE WRITING

In whole language classrooms, starting in Kindergarten, children write about their experiences and observations in journals. The blind child should be writing along with everyone else, using a Braillewriter or slate and stylus. Often the sighted children use a notebook for journal writing. The blind child can use sheets of Braille paper which can then be stapled together or placed in a folder or binder. Explain to your child that when the teacher says, "Take out your journals," your child should take out a sheet of Braille paper and insert it into the Braillewriter.

Students in whole language classrooms are usually encouraged to write down their thoughts and ideas and not to let the fact that they can't spell all the words they want to use get in the way. They are instructed to sound out any words they don't know how to spell and just keep writing. (This technique is referred to by names such as "invented spelling" and "kid spell.") The blind child should be encouraged in exactly the same way.

In Kindergarten and even first grade, many children must interpret their misspelled writings for the teacher, who then rewrites what they have written with the correct spellings at the bottom of the page. The same should be done for the child who writes in

THE BRIDGE TO BRAILLE

Braille. The teacher's rewriting is usually done in both Braille and print. In this way, the child can see the correct Braille and sighted teachers and family members can enjoy what the child has written.

In whole language classrooms, reading and writing are often combined and might be taught in many sessions and in all subjects over the course of the day. The blind child should have his/her writing tool/s wherever students will be expected to write. This might mean moving the Braillewriter around the classroom or taking it to different classrooms or even outdoors!

CORRECTING AND EDITING

It is helpful for a blind child to learn to work as accurately as possible, since correcting mistakes can mean a lot of re-Brailling. One way to avoid time-consuming rewriting is to check each sentence after writing it. (Don't teach the child to check each word; this slows the child down too much.) When a child finds a mistake, he/she can "erase" it by flattening the dots with a fingernail or a Braille eraser (a small wooden device with a narrow tip), or he/she can "cross it out" by writing over the error with full cells (also called the *f-o-r* sign), made by pressing all six keys at the same time. If your child chooses to use full cells, teach him/her always to use more than one so

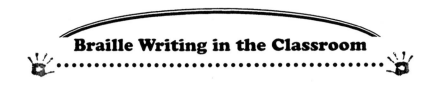

that the crossed out section will not be mistaken for the word *for*. Have your child practice correcting mistakes quickly so that he/she can work speedily in class.

Wikki Stix can be a terrific editing tool. The teacher or child can use small pieces of it to mark mistakes or sections to be rewritten on a first draft. (Use scissors to snip pieces to the desired size.) The child can then remove each piece as he/she writes the second draft. (Don't let any Wikki Stix get into the Braillewriter!) Teachers can also indicate errors with a small dab of GluColors, Hi Marks, or anything else which provides a tactual mark for the child to check when he/she gets the paper back.

Workbook Pages

It's a good idea to teach a child to "scan" a workbook page before beginning it, to get a sense of what the page consists of and its layout. As the child becomes accustomed to the different layouts in his/her various books, he/she will become speedier and more independent in doing the work.

Here is something to consider when a child is working on a workbook page. The Braille workbook will have the same questions as the print workbook, but the print page might have blank lines after each question, which indicate how long an answer is expected. For example, a short blank line after the question might mean that a one-word answer is expected; four lines extending all the way across the page would indicate that full sentences are required. The Braille book will not contain these lines. There might be a single full cell (*f-o-r* sign) for any length answer or there might be no indication at all. Initially someone can provide this information to the blind student; eventually he/she will remember that it might be given in the print version and will find out for him/herself.

MARKING ANSWERS

At times the child will need to mark answers, and not actually write them in Braille. He/she might also need to plot graphs, take polls, match answers, hold a place on a page, etc. An assortment of materials can be used for these tasks.

- For a matching task, the items could be Brailled on index cards; the child could then match the cards.
- The child might use a pencil or crayon (blind children should learn to draw lines, circle, and underline).
- To mark answers, the child could also use small pieces of Wikki Stix (use scissors to snip pieces to the desired size), push pins (the paper would be attached to a corkboard), magnets (with the

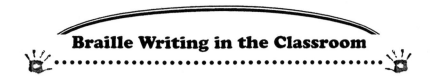
Braille Writing in the Classroom

paper attached to a magnet board), or the Swail Dot Inverter.
- For multiple choice tests, the child can flatten the dots of all the choices that are incorrect (although this method makes it hard to change an answer).

There are advantages and disadvantages to these techniques. Marking with a pencil or crayon is quick, but does not allow the child to check his/her work. Marking with Wikki Stix, the Swail, magnets, and pushpins allows the child to check his/her work and make corrections or changes, but probably takes more time than using pencil or crayon. When a child marks with magnets or pushpins, he/she cannot save the work to take home. Marking with Wikki Stix enables the child to check or correct his/her work and also save it to take home. If your child uses Wikki Stix for marking, however, he/she must learn how to press it on quite firmly or else the pieces will fall off.

If parents and teachers are aware of the various items available, they can expose the child to them and show him/her how to use them. Initially, the adults will probably decide what to use when, but it's a good idea to get the child involved with the decision making as soon as possible. The goal is for the child to know what is available and to be able to decide what will work best in each situation.

THE BRIDGE TO BRAILLE

SPELLING AND SPELLING TESTS

Some words are whole-word contractions in Braille. For example, *could* is written as *cd*; *work* is written *dot 5, w*; *little* is *ll*; *across* is *acr*. Since Braille books are written in Grade 2 (contracted) Braille (see A Quick Braille Lesson, page 13), your child will never see these words spelled out in his/her reading. Therefore, the actual spellings of these words must be specifically taught. For example, make sure your child knows that the word *could* is spelled *c-o-u-l-d* and *little* is spelled *l-i-t-t-l-e*. This will be important for spelling tests and for being able to type the words correctly later in life. Of course your child will also need know how to write the contractions correctly in Braille.

Give your child practice spelling out and writing such words. Well-developed memory skills will help your child in spelling (and in many other areas of life). Braille teachers often recommend writing spelling words both in their contracted and spelled-out forms for spelling homework and on tests.

TAKING NOTES

Note-taking skills are often introduced in the elementary grades. A blind student takes notes in much the same way as a sighted student. The only difference is that while a sighted student might work

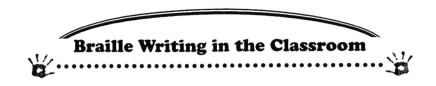

Braille Writing in the Classroom

in a notebook, a blind student will write on Braille paper and then place the sheets in a binder or folder.

When your child needs to create note cards for a report, he/she can simply use index cards in a Braillewriter or with a slate and stylus. (Braille users often use large index cards so that they can fit more words on each card.) Taking notes on cards is a flexible method all students can use for organizing information, creating an outline, or giving an oral report.

DOING MATH IN BRAILLE

DOING MATH IN BRAILLE

NEMETH CODE

Nemeth Code is the system of writing math in Braille. It was developed by a blind professor of mathematics, Dr. Abraham Nemeth, to make it possible to write any kind of mathematical notation, even the most complex, in Braille. Nemeth Code contains Braille symbols for every possible kind of mathematical and scientific notation. All math in Braille math books is written in Nemeth Code.

Nemeth Code numbers are shaped just like their literary counterparts, which blind children generally learn first (see A Quick Braille Lesson, page 13), so the Nemeth numbers are easy to recognize and read. The Nemeth numbers, however, are formed using the lower part of the Braille cell, dots 2, 3, 5, and 6.

The Nemeth Code Cheat Sheet at the end of this chapter explains how to write the math signs your child is likely to encounter in elementary school.

The Bridge to Braille

Getting Started with Numbers

Children will be introduced to literary numbers first, but they need to be familiar with reading and writing both literary and Nemeth Code numbers by the end of Kindergarten, so that when they begin addition and subtraction (which will be written in Nemeth Code in their math books and worksheets), they will be ready.

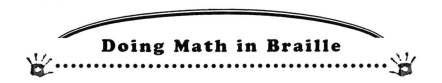

Doing Math in Braille

Children can begin learning to recognize numbers as preschoolers. If you feel your child is ready to learn numbers, you can make flashcards for him/her. Here's how: Mark the top of each card with a line of Braille *g*'s so the child will know which way to hold the card. Then Braille both the literary and Nemeth number on the card. Use the number sign (dots 3, 4, 5, 6) before the numbers; there is no space between the number sign and the number. Write the number in print above the Braille.

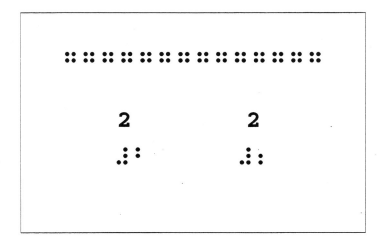

A number line taped to the child's desk in school can also be useful. A number line for literary numbers can be made with a Braille labeler (Braille labelers can only form literary numbers, not Nemeth numbers). To write Nemeth numbers, you can use the labeling tape attachment for the Braillewriter or a slate with slots for labeling tape. You can also Braille the numbers

THE BRIDGE TO BRAILLE

onto regular Braille paper or a self-stick plastic sheet, such as a laminating sheet, rolled into the Braillewriter (see Resources, pages 143 and 144). Cut off the strip of numbers and attach it to the child's desk.

MATH READINESS

Just as there are many skills that lead up to reading, there are also readiness skills that lead up to a child's being able to add, subtract, and perform more complex math operations. Learning to recognize the numbers and to count are important readiness skills, but in addition, your child will need lots of experience with other concepts:

- "One of," "two of," "a few," "several," "many," etc.
- How things compare with each other—more vs. less, a lot vs. a few, longer vs. shorter, thinner vs. wider, heavier vs. lighter, etc.
- Understanding that the number one refers to one thing, two refers to two things, three refers to three, etc.

Give your child lots of practice. For example, make up number games. Count out the forks for dinner together—"One for Mommy, one for Daddy, one for you, one for Brother;" or when you're cooking together, say, "Give me one potato and two carrots;" or as you are playing, say "I'll put two blocks in the container; you put three in."

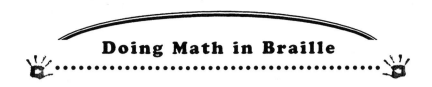

Doing Math in Braille

Count many things around the house—how many barrettes are in the container, how many cups are on the table, how many toy cars are in the basket, etc. You can also work with Unifix Cubes, a wonderful math teaching aid available at educational toy stores that can be used to introduce or practice many math concepts. These interlocking cubes will stay put when the child stacks them. They are color coded and can easily be tactually coded, too, with small pieces of self-stick felt, cork, plastic, foam, Velcro, and Wikki Stix.

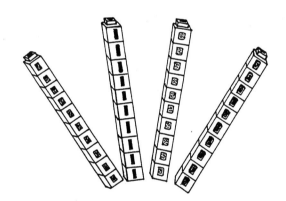

Unifix Cubes can easily be adapted with various self-stick textures

BEGINNING ADDITION AND SUBTRACTION

After your child has learned to read and write the numbers, he/she will begin adding and subtracting. At this point, the Braille teacher and the classroom teacher will be in very close contact. (Many teachers schedule a regular weekly meeting time in which to exchange

THE BRIDGE TO BRAILLE

information.) The classroom teacher will alert the Braille teacher to the new concepts and skills that will be coming up, so that the Braille teacher can teach the new Braille signs—such as plus, minus, and equals—to the blind student *before* the lesson is introduced in class. In this way, when the classroom teacher teaches that lesson, the child will be familiar with the new signs and will be able to read them.

Braille users usually learn how to set up both horizontal and vertical math problems on their own papers as soon as this kind of problem is introduced in school (usually first grade). (Print users at this point are usually only writing in the answers on their workbook pages and do not begin writing out problems on their papers until a good deal later.) The Braille teacher will teach your child an efficient method to follow in setting up math problems and a reliable method for keeping the fingers in the correct column when adding numbers with two or more digits.

As your child becomes used to setting up and working problems using the methods taught, he/she will begin to work faster and faster. The steps involved will become automatic. Soon your child will have a quick, efficient method that produces accurate, correctly spaced, neat work. Early work of this kind also prepares your Braille user for setting up problems in higher math—algebra, geometry, calculus, etc.—later in life.

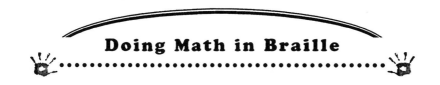

Doing Math in Braille

Other Beginning Math Concepts

When your child is learning to tell time, he/she can use a tactile learning clock and raised-line clock faces on paper, which are available from the American Printing House for the Blind (see Resources, page 154). You can also purchase a teaching clock from an educational supplies store and adapt it for tactile use. Braille the numbers 1 to 12 using a Braille labeler; use self-stick Velcro to mark the five-minute (hour) lines; use small snips of Wikki Stix for the other minute lines.

Blind children have no particular difficulty learning geometric and fraction concepts. These concepts, however, may be difficult for a beginner to grasp using only the raised-line drawings that appear in Brailled math books. It is better if the child can hold and examine geometric shapes and fraction pieces.

Sets of geometric shapes and various kinds of fraction kits are available from the American Printing House for the Blind and in educational supplies stores and catalogues. The fraction pieces can usually be adapted with Braille labels. If possible, supply your child with several kinds of fraction kits—fraction pies, fraction bars, etc.—so that he/she can experience fractions expressed in various ways, just as sighted children do.

WHAT DO MATH EXAMPLES LOOK LIKE IN BRAILLE?

As you look at your child's math work, you will see that math examples in Braille look very much like their print counterparts and are easily recognizable.

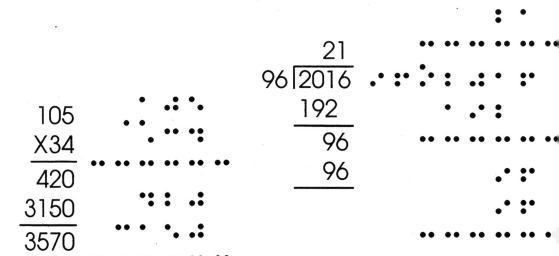

Doing Math in Braille

Some of the skills your child will learn as he/she begins to do math on paper will be specific to Braille:
- How to read and write the various math signs—plus, minus, times, divided by, equals, is greater than, is less than, etc.—in Braille
- How to space the numbers and signs correctly
- When to use the number sign
- How to determine when the embossing head of the Braillewriter is lined up in the correct column
- How to keep the fingers in the correct column when solving the problem

The layout and the actual figuring of the math IS EXACTLY THE SAME AS IN PRINT!

WRITING HORIZONTAL PROBLEMS

To write out a horizontal problem:

Begin with the number sign and first number (no space in between)

Write the plus, minus, times, or divided by sign (no space before or after)

Write second number (no number sign)

Space—equal sign—space (note: equal sign is a two-cell sign; write dots 4, 6, then dots 1, 3)

Number sign and answer (no space in between)

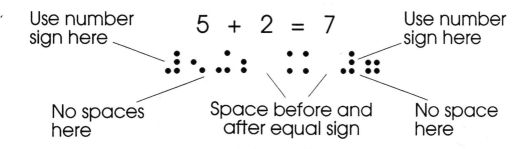

WRITING VERTICAL PROBLEMS

Vertical problems also require proper spacing. Here are the general guidelines for setting up vertical problems:

- Space several times after the example number so that there will be enough room for all columns in the example and in the answer.
- Leave plenty of space above, below, and next to each problem (the Braille teacher will teach your child a method for this).
- Do not use number signs in vertical problems.
- No lines are skipped within vertical problems.
- As with vertical problems written in print, columns in Braille problems must be lined up; that is, ones columns in the example with the ones column in the answer, tens columns with tens columns, hundreds with hundreds, etc.
- The plus or minus sign appears one cell to the left of the widest number in the example, on the line above the separation line (therefore, there may or may not be space between the plus or minus sign and the number that follows it).
- The multiplication sign is written immediately to the left of the multiplier (no space between the multiplication sign and the number that follows it).

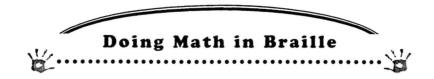
Doing Math in Braille

- The separation line between the example and the answer gets a line of its own.
- The separation line extends one cell beyond the example on the left and on the right.
- Decimal points will line up just as they do in print (when working multiplication problems involving decimals, the blind student must first figure out how many decimal places there will be in the answer, and then leave a blank cell in each partial product, above the place where the decimal point will be in the final product).
- The layout of the problem and figuring the actual math ARE EXACTLY THE SAME as in print!

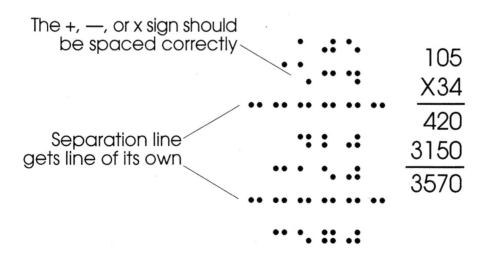

The +, —, or x sign should be spaced correctly

```
  105
  X34
  ───
  420
 3150
 ────
 3570
```

Separation line gets line of its own

Use no number signs   No skipped lines

THE BRIDGE TO BRAILLE

LONG DIVISION

Blind children love doing long division in Braille just as much as sighted children love doing it in print! Yes, long division takes a lot of time, but as you will see, the process in Braille IS EXACTLY THE SAME as in print, and listening to your child complain will no doubt bring back fond memories of your own long division days!

Here is a method for setting up long division:

Line space down four lines

Write the divisor (no number signs in long division)

Write the division sign right after the divisor—no space in between (just as in print, you must use the long division sign, not the one for horizontal problems)

Write the dividend (the number that is going to be divided) right after the division sign (no space between the division sign and the dividend)

Go up one line to write the separation line

Begin the separation line in the column containing the division sign and extend it one cell to the right of the dividend

The working of the problem—dividing, multiplying, subtracting, repeating the process, etc.—IS THE SAME AS IN PRINT

If the problem contains decimals, the blind student should either leave a space or write a decimal point in each partial product

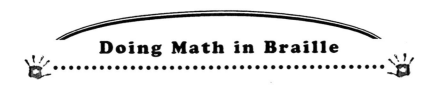

Doing Math in Braille

To write a remainder, go back to the quotient (answer) line, space once, then write a capital or lower case R (as the teacher has instructed the class) followed by dot 5 and then the remainder number (no number sign)

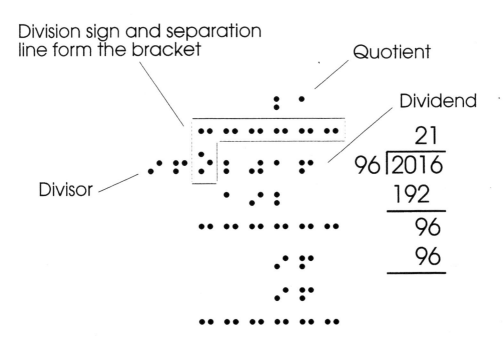

Use no number signs   No skipped lines

MUST MY CHILD WRITE OUT ALL THAT MATH?

As mentioned earlier, print users in the early grades generally write their answers right onto their workbook pages. They do not begin to write out the examples on their own papers until whatever year

their math book series switches to hardcover books. In contrast, Braille users are usually taught to write out the examples on their own papers starting in first grade.

Writing Answers onto the Workbook Page

There are several reasons why Braille teachers recommend that blind students learn how to set up the examples on their own paper right away, instead of Brailling the answers onto the Braille worksheet. If a page is removed from the Braille workbook, it needs to be trimmed evenly before it will go into the Braillewriter smoothly. Squashed Braille can also be a problem. Although it is possible to roll the Braille math page into the Braillewriter, there is usually not enough space between rows of examples for the child to Braille in the answers. The answer for one problem often ends up looking like a number to be added into the problem below! Also, it can be difficult, especially for a beginner, to align the embossing head of the Braillewriter in exactly the right position under the example to be worked. For all these reasons, Braille teachers usually recommend that the child learn how to write out the examples.

This means that the first grade Braille user will be doing work that is a little more advanced than his/her print-using classmates, but by third or fourth grade, when the print users are also writing out their

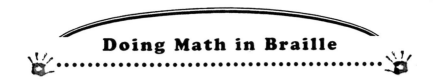

Doing Math in Braille

examples, the blind child will be comfortable with the skill and able to do it quickly.

If the child *is* going to write in the answers on the workbook page, someone will probably have to prepare the pages for the Braillewriter by evenly trimming the left edge. For an older student who can handle a binder, someone could trim the pages, punch holes on the left, and place the pages in order in a three-ring binder for the child to use independently.

Using an Answer Sheet

Another way to handle math is to use an answer sheet. However, using an answer sheet also requires more advanced skills than the average first or second grader is expected to have. Using an answer sheet might work well for older students, but it has two main disadvantages for young children. First, it is difficult for a young beginner to keep track of which example he/she is on in the book, especially if only the rows, and not every example, are numbered. To work successfully with an answer sheet, the child must be taught an efficient method for keeping the place. This could be done with a small piece of Wikki Stix (the child places the piece of Wikki Stix under the example being worked) or with the Stokes place holder (a metal board is inserted behind the page the child is working on; the child places a small magnet

just below the example being worked). (See Resources, page 144.)

The second disadvantage to using an answer sheet in the early grades is even more important. In first and second grade, children are learning about the ones column, the tens column, and the hundreds column. They are just learning that the columns in the example have a relationship to the columns in the answer. Seeing these relationships is especially important when two-digit adding and subtracting is introduced and when the class learns to do addition and subtraction with "regrouping" (your child's school might call this "trading," "renaming," "carrying," "borrowing," or some other name). Using an answer sheet does not allow the child to see these relationships. If the child is unable to see the problem as a whole because the example is on one sheet and the answer on another, it might interfere with his/her understanding of the concepts. Although writing out the whole problem might take longer at first, it does ensure that the child sees the problem as a whole.

Dictating Answers

While the young Braille student is still learning how to set up math examples on paper, the Braille teacher may suggest that he/she set up only three or four examples and then read the rest and dictate the answers to the teacher.

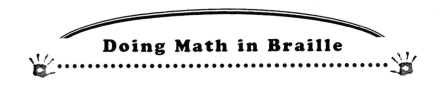

Doing Math in Braille

Using the Abacus

Another method for handling math work is to use the abacus. Sometimes the abacus is introduced as a fast way to compute without writing the whole problem out. However, since modern math teachers emphasize the *process* by which students derive an answer and not just the answer itself, they often want to see the students' work written out. For a full discussion of the advantages and disadvantages of the abacus, as well as for instruction in "The Paper-Compatible Abacus," see *Handbook for Itinerant and Resource Teachers of Blind and Visually Impaired Students*, listed in Resources, page 148.)

The Bottom Line

Whatever method is decided upon, it is essential that your Braille user *get the same experience with doing math* that his/her sighted classmates get. It is also extremely important that he/she *learn efficient, reliable systems* for doing the math. As the child gets older and becomes more proficient at doing all kinds of schoolwork, he/she will decide which way to do the work, sometimes choosing to write out the problems, sometimes using an answer sheet, sometimes writing in the answers on the workbook page, sometimes using an abacus, and usually using a great deal of mental math. Flexibility is important. Evaluate and

The Bridge to Braille

reevaluate the situation frequently and teach the child to do that, too. Give the child the tools to do the work in various ways and eventually he or she will decide which method is best for the task at hand.

Should the Workload Be Cut Down?

Sometimes Braille teachers suggest cutting down the number of examples the blind child will be responsible for. They say this based on the idea that it takes much longer to do math work in Braille. You might hear such statements as, "We generally suggest the work be cut in half for Braille students," or "Assign just the even numbers or every other row." Sometimes teachers say, "If she has demonstrated that she understands the concept, she shouldn't have to do every example." Unfortunately, this point of view often translates into *lowered expectations* for the blind student.

Many students can demonstrate an understanding of the work long before they finish every example. But this is true for sighted children as well as blind children. Blind students need and deserve as much exposure to the work as sighted students get. If the rest of the class is expected to complete the entire assignment, the blind child should do it, too. The goal is for the blind child to participate fully and equally in class.

• 110 •

Doing Math in Braille

Braille users are just as capable as print users at getting the job done! It may at times take a Braille user longer to complete certain assignments, but in general, the Braille user can handle the normal volume of work, especially if he/she has been taught efficient methods for doing the various tasks. Think about the future—in order to hold a good job, your child will need to be able to complete the work assigned!

If a child is taking an excessive amount of time to complete assignments, of course his/her general well-being must be taken into account—time for play and relaxation is important, too. You might find that it would make sense to shorten certain assignments for a time. Look at the whole situation. Try to make a good decision. And work at getting your child up to speed!

THE BRIDGE TO BRAILLE

NEMETH CODE CHEAT SHEET

Nemeth numbers

1　2　3　4　5　6　7　8　9　0

Number sign — dots 3, 4, 5, 6

100　　　1000　　　10,000

No space between number sign and number; use number sign only once in multi-digit numbers

Plus (+) — dots 3, 4, 6

No space before or after in horizontal problems; place one space to the left of widest number in vertical problems

Minus (—) — dots 3, 6

No space before or after in horizontal problems; place one space to the left of widest number in vertical problems

Times (×) — dot 4; dots 1, 6

No space before or after in horizontal problems; place just to left of multiplier in vertical problems no space

Divided by ( ) — dots 4, 6; dots 3, 4

No space before or after in horizontal problems

Equals (=) — dots 4, 6; dots 1, 3

Space before and after

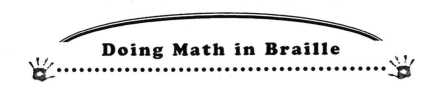

Doing Math in Braille

Separation line	⠒⠒⠒⠒	dots 2, 5
Gets line of its own; extends one space to left and right of widest number in problem		
Long division	⠒⠒⠒⠒⠒ ⠭	dots 2, 5 dots 1, 3, 5
Write division sign as you write the problem; separation line begins just above division sign on its own line and extends one space to the right of the dividend		
Comma	⠠	dot 6
Notice that Nemeth comma is different dot from literary comma (dot 2); no space before or after		
Cent sign (¢)	⠈⠉	dot 4; dots 1, 4
Write number sign, number, and cent sign; no space between last digit of number and cent sign		
Dollar sign ($)	⠈⠎	dot 4; dots 2, 3, 4
Write dollar sign, then number; no space between dollar sign and number; do not use number sign		
Decimal point	⠨	dots 4, 6
No space before or after		
Greater than (>)	⠨⠂	dots 4, 6; dot 2
Space before and after		
Less than (<)	⠐⠅	dot 5; dots 1, 3
Space before and after		

THE BRIDGE TO BRAILLE

Not equal to (⟩) Space before and after	⠙ ⠻ ⠁	dots 3, 4; dots 4, 6; dots 1, 3
Fraction indicator opening	⠹	dots 1, 4, 5, 6
Fraction indicator closing	⠼	dots 3, 4, 5, 6
Fraction line	⠌	dots 3, 4
Example: $\frac{1}{3}$	⠹⠁⠌⠉⠼	
Mixed number indicator opening	⠸⠹	dots 4, 5, 6; dots 1, 4, 5, 6
Mixed number indicator closing	⠸⠼	dots 4, 5, 6; dots 3, 4, 5, 6
Example: $2\frac{1}{3}$	⠼⠃⠸⠹⠁⠌⠉⠸⠼	
Percent (%)	⠨⠴	dot 4; dots 3, 5, 6
Write number sign, number, percent sign; no space between last digit of number and percent sign		
Tally marks	⠸	dots 4, 5, 6
Example: ЖЖ II	⠸ ⠸ ⠸ ⠸ ⠸ ⠸ ⠸ ⠸	

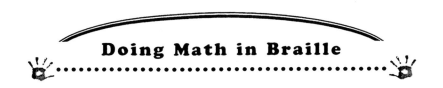

Doing Math in Braille

Roman numerals capitals

When writing capital Roman numerals of just one letter (such as I, V, X, etc.), write dots 5, 6, then the capital sign (dot 6), then the letter of the Roman numeral

Example: V

For capital Roman numerals of more than one letter (such as III, VII, IX, etc.) use the double capital sign (dot 6; dot 6), then write the Roman numerals

Example: VII

Roman numerals lower case

When writing lower case Roman numerals of any length (such as i, ii, viii, etc.) write dots 5, 6, then the Roman numeral

Example: iii

Example numbers

Example numbers in math books are written using Nemeth numbers. Write number sign, number, punctuation indicator (dots 4, 5, 6), period

Example: 4.

Time

Write the number sign, then the hour number, a punctuation indicator (dots 4, 5, 6), a colon (dots 2, 5), another number sign, and then the minutes

Example: 5:45

• 115 •

INDEPENDENCE IN THE CLASSROOM

Independence in the Classroom

There are many possible ways to set up the child's classroom work area, but always strive for a system that maximizes independence and a seating placement that ensures full participation.

Desk Size and Placement

The child will need a large surface area that can accommodate the Braillewriter, a Braille book, an answer sheet, and perhaps a tray for "manipulatives," the math counters and other small items often used in primary classrooms. An L-shaped set-up or a larger than usual desk (approximately 30" x 50") can work well. If for some reason teachers feel the desk must be located in a certain area of the room, *make sure the child is not placed in an isolated spot.* It is absolutely essential that the blind child be seated with the other children, able to socialize and be a real part of the class. If an aide is assisting in the classroom, make sure the child's desk is set up for the *child's* use, not the aide's! (In fact, it's probably best if the aide's area is in another part of the classroom entirely, away from the blind student.)

THE BRIDGE TO BRAILLE

ARRANGING MATERIALS AND EQUIPMENT

The child's books, folders, notebooks, Braille paper, etc., should be in logical places within the child's easy reach. He/she needs to know where they are and needs to be able to get them independently. An expandable vertical file with several slots (from an office supplies store) works well for holding these items. Notebooks and folders can be labeled in Braille for quick locating. Place the label tape where the title of a Braille book would be (on the front cover, upper left, parallel to the binding, words facing the binding), so it is easy to find and read with the fingers. Horizontal stacking trays (like an office in-box) are another option. Each tray can be labeled and folders and papers can be placed in them.

Since the Braille versions of your child's textbooks can contain many volumes, it might be best to have only the volume in use of each textbook at the child's desk. This will make it easier for the child to get out his/her books and find pages quickly.

Your child's Braillewriter will probably be on the desk all the time. A felt pad placed beneath the Braillewriter makes it easy to push the Braillewriter to the back of the desk when it is not needed and to pull it back again when it is. A rubber pad or rectangle of Dycem (see Resources, page 143) placed on the desk next to the Braillewriter keeps papers and books from

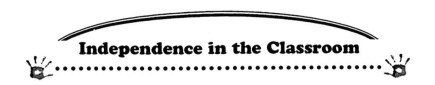

Independence in the Classroom

slipping. A tray with raised edges or a large box lid can be kept nearby to hold "manipulatives." The tray can be used as a work surface when the child is using these small objects; it will keep them from falling off the desk. Small paper cups or film cans can be fastened to the desk with Fun-Tak (see Resources, page 145) in convenient places to hold pushpins, magnets, paper clips, Braille name labels, snips of Wikki Stix, etc.

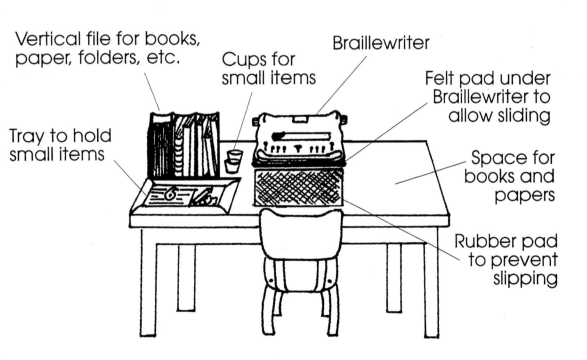

The Bridge to Braille

Keeping Paperwork in Order

Your child needs a convenient system for organizing papers and bringing homework back and forth to school. The child can use a binder–label a section in Braille for each subject or for homework, worksheets, finished papers, etc. An oversized pocket folder, 12 ½" x 12 ½", large enough to accommodate 11 ½" x 11" Braille workbook pages, also works. Oversized plastic folders are available from American Printing House for the Blind (see Resources, page 154).

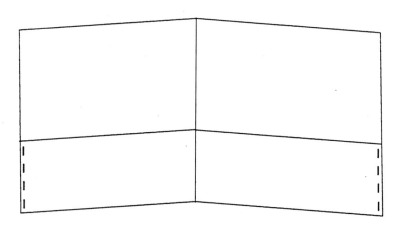

You can make a large pocket folder from a piece of posterboard–fold the posterboard in half; fold the bottom up to form the pockets; trim to 12 ½"; staple edges; cover staples with heavy tape.

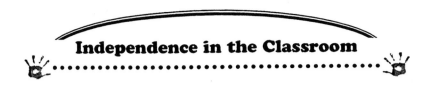
Independence in the Classroom

To carry books and papers back and forth to school, your child needs a large enough bookbag. A large tote bag (16" x 16") or backpack (18" tall x 15" wide) can accommodate Braille books and large folders.

LAYING THE GROUNDWORK FOR INDEPENDENCE

It is up to the adults in a blind student's life to set up systems for the child to use. This is done for sighted students automatically—we don't even think about it! For example, bookbags are sized to fit print books; ordinary desktops can easily accommodate the papers and materials a sighted student would use. It is the adults' job to create such efficient, well-organized, easy-to-use systems for the blind student.

When provided with and taught good methods of organization, a blind student will be able to work efficiently and independently. Initially someone will help the child learn and use these systems. Over time, the blind student needs to develop both the skills and the responsibility to use these systems independently. Since the responsibility must ultimately be transferred to the child, parents and teachers must build the transfer into the child's training. This training will enable the child eventually to create and use efficient systems by him/herself, an outcome desired for any child.

USING TECHNOLOGY

USING TECHNOLOGY

A great deal of technology now exists which can be utilized by blind learners. Computers can be made to "talk"; Braille "printers" can produce Braille from what is typed on an ordinary computer keyboard; reading machines can read print books aloud. Your child may use all or just a little of this technology.

Is this technology *essential* for a blind child's success in school? No, or at least no more so than for sighted students. Braille is essential; the ability to read and write is essential. The important thing to remember is that *technology does not replace literacy.*

Can technology be sensibly used to *enhance* a child's education? Yes! Braille and speech computer output, for instance, can make it easy for a blind student to check his/her work independently and hand in assignments in print. Braille-to-print devices make it possible for a teacher to read in print what the child is Brailling. And, of course, as technology

becomes more and more a part of everyone's everyday life, the blind child needs and deserves the same exposure to it and training in it as the other children in the class receive.

An Overview of High-Tech Devices
Computer Access

To make a computer accessible for a blind user, two components are needed: **screen reading software** (also called screen access software) and **speech or Braille hardware**. (Speech *software* that uses the computer's sound card is becoming available.) This equipment enables the blind user to use a computer independently. It is available for IBM and Apple or Macintosh desktop and laptop computers. The software reads screen messages as well as what is being/has been typed. It allows flexible reading by the document, page, paragraph, sentence, line, word, or individual letter.

Speech Access—To make a computer "talk," the computer must be equipped with a screen reading program and either an internal or external speech synthesizer or speech software that works with a sound card. The speech can be set to announce each key stroke for beginning typists. Earphones can be connected for quiet use.

Braille Access—For Braille access to the screen, the computer must have screen reading software and

Using Technology

a "refreshable Braille" (also called "paperless Braille") display. A refreshable Braille display consists of a line of cells in which Braille is formed by pins which rise and fall. It is called "refreshable" because the arrangement of pins changes with each keystroke or as the cursor is moved. The Braille display shows, in Braille, screen messages and what is being/has been typed. The Braille display unit is designed so that, when the keyboard is placed upon it, both the keyboard and the display are easily accessible.

Advantages of Computer Use: Motivating, fun. Makes editing and rewriting easy. Typing and word processing are extremely useful skills for blind learners. Any sighted teacher can read the screen to see what the child is writing. Can be used with print or Braille printers to get hard copy.

Disadvantages: Does not keep up Braille writing skills (important for younger children). Desktop models are not portable—would restrict where the child could work.

Advantages of Speech Access: A relatively inexpensive way to achieve access to screen information. Many children enjoy computer voices.

Disadvantages: Not as precise as refreshable Braille for proofreading.

THE BRIDGE TO BRAILLE

Advantages of Braille Access: Many blind computer users report working more efficiently when they can read their work in Braille rather than just listen to it. Refreshable Braille is more precise than speech for proofreading.

Disadvantages: Very expensive; somewhat fragile. Because of cost, most displays are small (40 or 80 cells) and can show only a half a line or one line at a time. (Blind users look forward to the day when there will be an affordable full-page Braille display.)

Braille "Printers"

Technically called Braille embossers, but commonly referred to as Braille printers, these devices produce Braille from what a person types on a computer keyboard or notetaker (see next page). **Braille translation software** is required to run a Braille printer.

Advantages: Provides access to much more Braille—teachers can Braille worksheets, last-minute items, short books, announcements, school menus, Valentine cards, etc. simply by typing on a computer keyboard. Anyone can use it; requires no knowledge of Braille. Teacher can use to type and Braille out comments, spelling corrections, etc., and staple them to child's written work; this enables blind student to get same feedback as sighted students. If computer is hooked up to both print and Braille printers, teacher can create assignments on computer and produce print copies for sighted class members and Braille copy for blind student.

When blind student uses computer, he/she can get Braille hard copy of work. If computer is hooked up to both print and Braille printers, student can get Braille copy for him/herself and print copy for the teacher.

Disadvantages: Loud when embossing.

Notetakers

Notetakers are small, lightweight, portable talking computer devices (such as the Braille 'n Speak and the Braillemate) made specifically for blind users. They have either a Braille or typewriter keyboard. They are useful for a variety of tasks such as writing, taking notes, and other basic word processing, and for keeping a calendar, recording phone numbers, etc. Notetakers can be cabled to print and Braille printers. Some notetakers are equipped with refreshable Braille (see Braille Access, page 128).

Advantages: Small, portable, quiet. Can easily be carried to different classrooms. Notetaker with Braille keyboard enables child to continue to get practice in Braille fingering, important in the early grades. If notetaker has refreshable Braille, student can read as well as listen to what has been written. Older students can download files onto a PC.

Disadvantages: Notetakers are paperless; no hard copy (paper copy) is produced at the time of writing. Therefore, unless the notetaker has refreshable Braille, the child cannot read back in Braille what has been written (he/she can listen to it, though). Notetakers are also screenless, so that a sighted teacher cannot check what the child is writing at that moment.

Braille-to-Print Devices for the Braillewriter

Braille-to-print devices translate what has been written on the Braillewriter into print. The device is attached to the Braillewriter and cabled to a printer.

Advantages: Enables teachers who do not know Braille to get an instant printout of what the child is Brailling; may eliminate the need to write print above the Braille on the child's papers.

Using Technology

Disadvantages: The printout can be difficult to understand if the child does not press the keys heavily enough, or erases and then writes over a word or crosses out a word on the Braillewriter. If the child goes back to edit a section, the change will appear at the end of the printout, rather than where it is in the original, also making the printout confusing. If you are using one of these devices, be sure to check the original Braille before you assume the child has made a mistake. Also, these devices cannot print out Nemeth Code, so they cannot be used for math.

Mountbatten Brailler

The Mountbatten is a multi-function device. It is an electronic Braillewriter; it can be cabled to a printer to produce a print copy of what has been Brailled; it can produce Braille from what is typed on a computer keyboard; and it can be used as a silent notetaker–the user Brailles directly into memory (no paper copy) for later retrieval.

Advantages: Student can produce both Braille and print copy of what has been Brailled; can be used in limited way as a Braille printer. Anyone can produce Braille by typing on the computer keyboard.

Disadvantages: If someone is using the device to produce Braille by typing on the keyboard, then the blind student cannot be using the machine for Brailling! The keyboard has no screen; therefore, the person typing on the keyboard connected directly to the device cannot see what is being typed. Expensive, compared to a manual Braillewriter; loud when Brailling/embossing.

CHOOSING HIGH-TECH EQUIPMENT

Blind students will use different equipment for different tasks and at different stages in their schooling. For example, a student might use a Braillewriter with a Braille-to-print device attached in the primary grades, a Braillewriter and a laptop equipped with speech and/or Braille in fifth and sixth grades, and then perhaps a notetaker in the later grades, when he/she changes classes every day.

Here are some questions you can ask yourself when you are figuring out which equipment would make sense for your child:

- What are my child's needs?
- What do I want to accomplish with this device?
- Are my child's literacy skills solid?
- Is cost an issue? Is adequate funding available?
- Where will the equipment be placed?

Using Technology

- Who will make sure all the components are compatible?
- Is training available in the use of the device for the student and the teachers?

Keep yourself informed of the advances in this technology, prioritize goals, and analyze what would be best for your child at that point in his/her schooling. Find out what the current education law says about the school's responsibility for funding adaptive equipment. Some community service organizations will help with the cost. Be prepared for some glitches; getting a system up and running can be a challenge.

Be flexible; often there will be more than one workable option for a situation. Remember that one piece of equipment will probably not answer all your child's needs. Encourage your child to be flexible, too; he/she must learn how to decide when to use which equipment! Lastly, realize that technology is not a magic solution if your child is having school problems.

To sample technological equipment, visit the enormous technology exhibit at the National Convention of the National Federation of the Blind, held in a different city each July. There, vendors exhibit not only what is currently available, but also items that are not even on the market yet! Another

THE BRIDGE TO BRAILLE

way to keep current is to visit the International Braille and Technology Center for the Blind in Baltimore, MD. The Technology Center is committed to having on display every piece of Braille technology that is available. The Technology Center's director will consult by telephone. Call the Technology Center at the number below for details on both of these exhibits.

Comprehensive evaluations of all Braille-related technology are available from the following sources:

INTERNATIONAL BRAILLE AND TECHNOLOGY
CENTER FOR THE BLIND
1800 JOHNSON ST.
BALTIMORE, MD 21230
(410) 659-9314
www.nfb.org

AMERICAN PRINTING HOUSE FOR THE BLIND
1839 FRANKFORT AVE.
PO BOX 6085
LOUISVILLE, KY 40206-0085
1-800-223-1839
www.aph.org

RESOURCES

Resources

Many items with the tactile and/or auditory qualities that work well with blind children can be easily found in discount stores, toy stores and catalogues, and educational supplies stores and catalogues. Look around the next time you are in one of these stores and let your creativity flow! You'll be amazed at how many of these readily available materials can be used with your child.

In addition to looking in regular stores and catalogues, get on mailing lists for catalogues that sell items made specifically for blind people. You will then be able to keep up to date on what's new in this specialized area. You'll get a kick out of many of these items, and often they will keep you from having to reinvent the wheel.

The Bridge to Braille

Helpful Items

The items listed in this section are arranged in the order in which they appear in the book. This means that items used for the same purpose are grouped together. Addresses for ordering begin on page 154.

Self-Stick Textures

Intended for use on bottom of lamps, bookends, statues, etc. to keep them from scratching furniture; available in felt, plastic bubble, foam, cork, etc. Can be used to adapt worksheets, make graphs, etc. Also can be used to mark items that feel similar (such as favorite tapes) so that the pre-reading child can identify items and get them independently.

- Available at hardware and discount stores

Velcro

Intended as a fastener, but self-stick Velcro can also be used to adapt materials as above; self-stick kind provides two different textures for adapting worksheets, Unifix cubes, games, etc.

- Available at discount stores, sewing supplies stores, etc.

Wooden Craft Pieces

Useful for adapting worksheets; attach with glue or double-sided tape.

- Available at craft supplies stores

Resources

Hi Marks

A special item made for blind people; thick, liquid tactile marker. Squeeze tube to write, draw, or make marks; leaves a feelable line when dry. Use in advance—must dry before blind child can touch line or mark.

↣ Available from Lighthouse Enterprises (page 155)

Elmer's GluColors

Colored glue that has a thicker consistency than regular glue; can be used to make raised-line drawings. Use in advance—must dry before blind student can touch drawing.

↣ Available at discount stores, stationery stores, supermarkets, etc.

Wikki Stix

A craft/art item made of waxed string; great for making raised-line drawings and outlining shapes; blind student can draw and decorate papers with it; small snips can be used for editing, making graphs, and marking answers, corrections, and unknown contractions, etc.

↣ Available at craft stores, educational toy stores, teacher supplies stores

Tracing Wheel

Intended as sewing tool; can be used to make raised-line drawings. Place paper wrong side up over rubber

THE BRIDGE TO BRAILLE

pad or pile of newspapers; trace along outlines with tracing wheel; feelable line will result on right side.

➻ Available at sewing supplies and discount stores

SWAIL DOT INVERTER

A special tool created for blind people; Braille paper is placed over a rubber pad; pressing the dot inverter stylus makes individual raised dots. Useful for making tactile drawings, charts, graphs, etc.; child can use to mark answers, fill in graphs, etc. Kit contains stylus and rubber pad.

➻ Available from American Printing House for the Blind (page 154)

SEWELL RAISED LINE DRAWING KIT

A special tool made for blind people; useful for creating raised-line drawings. Kit contains clipboard, plastic sheets, stylus.

➻ Available from Lighthouse Enterprises (page 155)

INDEX CARDS

Roll into Braillewriter to make flashcards for blind student; older student can use large cards in Braillewriter or with slate and stylus to take notes for reports.

➻ Available at discount stores, stationery stores, office supplies stores, supermarkets, etc.

Resources

BRAILLE LABELER

Labeler which produces Braille on self-stick plastic tape; dial has both print and Braille letters. Useful for labeling items, making graphs, putting teacher's comments on blind student's papers, marking on/off keys on calculators, etc. Labels with student's name can be used for classroom mailbox, library check-out cards, art projects, etc.

- Available from Materials Center, National Federation of the Blind (page 155)

LABELING TAPE ATTACHMENT FOR BRAILLEWRITER

Metal plate with clips to hold labeling tape; fits onto Braillewriter. Slide labeling tape under two clips; Braille as usual onto tape.

- Available from Howe Press (page 154)

SLATE WITH SLOTS FOR LABELING TAPE

Insert labeling tape into slots; Braille as usual.

- Available from Howe Press (page 154)

DYCEM

A rubbery non-slip surface; child can use at home and at school to keep plastic book pages, flashcards, papers, playing cards, etc. from sliding. Sold in rolls and as individual placemats.

- Available from North Coast Medical, 187 Stauffer Blvd., San Jose, CA 95125-1042; 1-800-821-9319; www.ncmedical.com

THE BRIDGE TO BRAILLE

LAMINATING SHEET

Clear plastic sheets with self-stick backing; useful for making Braille number line for desk, adapting games, Brailling short books (place clear Brailled plastic sheet right over print), etc.

- Available at stationery and office supplies stores

UNIFIX CUBES

Math teaching aid; cubes fit together easily and stay put; color-coded cubes can easily be coded for tactile use with various self-stick textures (see above). This wonderful aid has many uses—to teach counting, one-to-one correspondence, putting together (addition and multiplication), taking apart (subtraction and division), grouping, comparing, graphing, solving word problems, and much more!

- Available from educational catalogues and toy stores

STOKES BRAILLE PLACE HOLDER

A special item made for blind people; consists of a metal board and magnets. Place metal board behind a page in a book; use magnet on the page to mark a place.

- Available from American Printing House for the Blind (page 154)

Resources

VERTICAL FILE OR HORIZONTAL STACKING TRAYS

Useful for keeping books and folders organized and in easy reach on child's desk; expandable.

➻ Available at office supplies stores

FUN-TAK

Reusable adhesive; does not leave residue; has many uses including attaching small items to child's desk.

➻ Available at discount, teacher supplies, office supplies, and stationery stores

THE BRIDGE TO BRAILLE

HELPFUL BOOKS

The books in this section are listed in the order in which they are mentioned in the text. A few additional books are included. Ordering information can be found in the Sources of Materials, Books, and Information section beginning on page 154.

JUST ENOUGH TO KNOW BETTER: A BRAILLE PRIMER
by Eileen P. Curran
from National Braille Press (page 152)

A warm, wonderful way to learn Braille. An easy way to keep one step ahead of your new Braille reader. In addition to easy-to-follow lessons and tips for learning Braille, the author includes two interesting essays as practice exercises—one by a parent of a blind child, the other by a blind adult.

BRAILLE CODES AND CALCULATIONS PLUS DOT WRITING: A SELF-STUDY KIT FOR TEACHERS, PARENTS AND PARAPROFESSIONALS
from Exceptional Teaching Aids (page 154)

Teaches the entire literary Braille code; gives symbols and formats of the Nemeth Code through sixth-grade math; introduces Braille music, computer, and foreign language codes. Includes information on using the Braillewriter, making worksheets for young students, and more.

Resources

Learning the Nemeth Braille Code: A Manual for Teachers and Students
by Ruth H. Craig
from American Printing House for the Blind (page 154)

Signs, symbols, spatial arrangements, formats, rules—everything you ever wanted to know about the Nemeth Code!

Tactual Discrimination Worksheets
from American Printing House for the Blind (page 154)

Worksheets provide activities designed to develop the ability to interpret tactile figures, forms, and lines, and to recognize Braille characters.

The Mangold Developmental Program of Tactile Perception and Braille Letter Recognition
from Exceptional Teaching Aids (page 154)

Worksheets develop tactile discrimination, proper hand position, rapid tracking across Braille line, and letter recognition. Also includes games and tests.

The Mangold Developmental Program of Tactile Perception and Nemeth Numeral Recognition
from Exceptional Teaching Aids (page 154)

Program introduces Braille numerals and teaches rapid and accurate Braille number recognition; provides practice in tracking numbers horizontally and vertically. Includes worksheets, games, tests, and more.

THE BRIDGE TO BRAILLE

Curriculum Guide for Braille Readiness

Discovering Braille: A Workbook for Beginning Readers

Discovering Braille: A Workbook of Special Signs

Learning to Read Braille Contractions

all by Michael Cerwinski

from Metropolitan NJ Chapter, American Red Cross, 2 Gardner Rd., Fairfield, NJ 07004; 1-800-783-4272; www.rcmetronj.org

Activities, materials, and evaluation suggestions for several methods of teaching Braille.

Handbook for Itinerant and Resource Teachers of Blind and Visually Impaired Students

by Doris M. Willoughby and Sharon L. M. Duffy

from National Federation of the Blind (page 155)

Comprehensive (533 pages!), detailed guide to the education of blind and visually impaired children. Written primarily for teachers but information is essential for parents, too. Includes detailed method for using *Patterns* series. Topics range from early childhood concept development to study skills, from map study to arts and crafts, from testing and evaluation to fitting in socially, from mathematics to phys ed, from home economics and daily living skills to power tools. A MUST HAVE book for parents.

Resources

PATTERNS: THE PRIMARY BRAILLE READING PROGRAM
from American Printing House for the Blind (page 154)

Reading program designed specifically for young beginning Braille readers, readiness through third reader level. Includes Braille texts and worksheets, teacher's edition with lesson plans, mastery tests, and supplementary worksheets. Library Series contains pleasure books at the various reading levels.

GUIDELINES AND GAMES FOR TEACHING EFFICIENT BRAILLE READING
by Myrna R. Olson
from American Foundation for the Blind (page 154)

Contains many ideas for preschoolers' development and literacy, exercises and ideas for beginning Braille readers, games to make Braille learning fun, a list of comprehension questions to check child's reading, assessments of reading and Braille skills, as well as remediation ideas for problem readers. Contains some negative attitudes towards Braille and outdated information on computers, but on the whole, a very worthwhile book to have.

A HANDBOOK OF BRAILLE CONTRACTIONS
compiled by Harry Schuchman
from American Action Fund for Blind Children and Adults (page 151)

An easy-to-use reference guide to Braille contractions and punctuation signs in Twin Vision format.

The Bridge to Braille

Twin Vision Dictionary of Braille Problem Words
compiled by Harry Schuchman and Marian Davidson
from American Action Fund for Blind Children and Adults (page 151)
A dictionary of Braille sticklers showing the words in proper contracted form.

The Burns Braille Transcription Dictionary
by Mary F. Burns
from American Foundation for the Blind (page 154)
A quick reference guide to Braille letters, contractions, punctuation, and composition symbols; sections display symbols and contractions alphabetically, with dot numbers and all meanings and rules.

The Oregon Project
by Donnise Brown, Vickie Simmons, Judy Methvin, Sharon Anderson, Sue Biogon, Kris Davis
from Jackson Education Service District, Attn: OR Project, 101 No. Grape St., Medford, OR 97501; 1-800-636-7450; www.jacksonesd.k12.or.us/speced/regionalserv/ORPROJ.htm

Comprehensive curriculum for blind children from birth to age six. Includes a skills inventory in cognitive, language, self-help, socialization, fine motor, gross motor, vision, and compensatory skills areas. Useful not only as an evaluation tool, but also as a source of ideas for activities.

Resources

SOURCES OF BRAILLE BOOKS

AMERICAN ACTION FUND FOR BLIND CHILDREN AND ADULTS
1800 JOHNSON ST.
BALTIMORE, MD 21230
(410) 659-9314
www.blindactionfund.org

Offers the Kenneth Jernigan Library for Blind Children, free by-mail national lending library of Twin Vision (Braille and print) and Braille books, including Great Document Series with works such as Declaration of Independence in Braille. Will send books to home and school. Sends free Braille calendar to those who apply for service. Provides newspaper service for deaf-blind people.

AMERICAN PRINTING HOUSE FOR THE BLIND (APH)
1839 FRANKFORT AVE.
PO BOX 6085
LOUISVILLE, KY 40206-0085
1-800-223-1839
www.aph.org

Major source of Braille textbooks, instructional materials, aids, tools, and supplies for blind people. APH also sells a limited number of Braille fiction books in their Century Series.

THE BRIDGE TO BRAILLE

CATHOLIC GUILD FOR THE BLIND
180 NORTH MICHIGAN AVE, #1700
CHICAGO, IL 60601-7463
(312) 236-8569
www.guildfortheblind.org

Offers tactile-picture coloring books, a book on making pictures using Braille dots, and some fiction books.

NATIONAL BRAILLE PRESS
88 ST. STEPHEN ST.
BOSTON, MA 02115
(617) 266-6160
1-800-548-7323
www.nbp.org

Publisher of Braille books, including children's print-Braille books, calendars, and a speller. Offers Braille Book Club for children from preschool to third grade. Membership is free.

NATIONAL LIBRARY SERVICE FOR THE BLIND AND
PHYSICALLY HANDICAPPED (NLS)
LIBRARY OF CONGRESS
1291 TAYLOR ST. NW
WASHINGTON, DC 20542
1-800-424-8567
www.loc.gov/nls

Provides Braille books through its network of state and regional libraries for the blind and physically handicapped. Books are sent free of charge through the mail to home and school. Also provides Braille music materials. Administers Braille transcribing course.

Resources

SEEDLINGS—BRAILLE BOOKS FOR CHILDREN
PO BOX 51924
LIVONIA, MI 48151-5924
1-800-777-8552
www.seedlings.org

Publishes Braille books which are sold at a reasonable cost. Seedlings offers print-Braille books for younger children and all-Braille books for older readers. Provides encyclopedia articles in Braille for student reports and projects free of charge.

VERY BUMPY STORIES
VOLUNTEER BRAILLE SERVICE
4139 REGENT AVE. NORTH
ROBBINSDALE, MN 55422
(763) 971-5231

Offers print-Braille books from preschool through elementary levels.

WILLIAM A. THOMAS BRAILLE BOOKSTORE
BRAILLE INTERNATIONAL, INC.
3290 S. E. SLATER ST.
STUART, FL 34997
1-800-336-3142
www.brailleintl.org

Produces and sells copies of some of the Braille books published by the National Library Service for the Blind and Physically Handicapped, for people who wish to purchase rather than borrow these books. Operates both mail order service and walk-in bookstore.

THE BRIDGE TO BRAILLE

SOURCES OF MATERIALS, BOOKS, AND INFORMATION

AMERICAN FOUNDATION FOR THE BLIND (AFB)
11 PENN PLAZA, SUITE 300
NY, NY 10001
1-800-232-3044
www.afb.org

Provides information and books about blindness.

AMERICAN PRINTING HOUSE FOR THE BLIND (APH)
1839 FRANKFORT AVE.
PO BOX 6085
LOUISVILLE, KY 40206-0085
1-800-223-1839
www.aph.org

Provides instructional materials, tools, and supplies.

EXCEPTIONAL TEACHING AIDS
20102 WOODBINE AVE.
CASTRO VALLEY, CA 94546
1-800-549-6999
www.exceptionalteaching.com

Provides materials for education, recreation, and independent living.

HOWE PRESS
PERKINS SCHOOL FOR THE BLIND
175 NO. BEACON ST.
WATERTOWN, MA 02472
(617) 924-3490
www.perkins/pvt.k12.ma.us

Produces Perkins Braillewriter, some math aids, and slates and styluses.

Resources

LIGHTHOUSE ENTERPRISES
CONSUMER PRODUCTS DIVISION
111 EAST 59TH ST., 12TH FL.
NEW YORK, NY 10022
1-800-829-0500
www.lighthouse.org

Provides materials for recreation and independent living.

NATIONAL FEDERATION OF THE BLIND (NFB)
1800 JOHNSON ST.
BALTIMORE, MD 21230
(410) 659-9314
www.nfb.org

Organization of blind people, families, and friends working for opportunity and equality for the blind. Materials Center provides information, literature, aids, appliances, and training. Publishes *The Braille Monitor*. Houses the International Braille and Technology Center for the Blind.

NATIONAL ORGANIZATION OF
PARENTS OF BLIND CHILDREN (NOPBC)
1800 JOHNSON ST.
BALTIMORE, MD 21230
(410) 659-9314
www.nfb.org

Works to create a climate of opportunity for blind and visually impaired children in home, school, and society. Provides information, support, resources, training, and national magazine *Future Reflections* for parents and teachers of blind children. Helps parents gain understanding of blindness through contact with blind adults. Local affiliates in all parts of country. Division of NFB.

APPENDICES

Literacy, Learning, and Louis Braille
by Agnes Allen

As a student at the Western Pennsylvania School for the Blind in Pittsburgh back in the 1930's and early 1940's B.C. (before computers), I learned to read and write Braille. Braille was a given in those days; it was basic to everything else I learned in school. All my textbooks were in Braille. Listening to a history or geography lesson on tape was unheard of. Oh, yes, talking books were available for listening enjoyment if I chose to go that route for entertainment and leisure-time activity. But for honest-to-goodness, hard-core study purposes there was no substitute for Braille for me as a blind child. And even my partially-sighted classmates had to learn Braille. Some of them were compelled to read with aprons tied around their necks, which covered their fingers as they moved across the page to prevent peeking at the dots. Looking back now, I wonder just how often those kids succumbed to the temptation to lift the apron for a peek at the dots when teacher was looking the other way. But seriously, for me the mastery of Braille was the key to becoming literate, just as print was for my fully sighted friends.

Agnes Allen has been a Braille reader for sixty-five years. She currently teaches Braille both as a private tutor and in the public schools. The text of this article was first presented at the 1996 State Convention of the National Federation of the Blind of NJ.

The Bridge to Braille

Because I was Braille-literate, I could go on to college to become an English major, reading Chaucer and Shakespeare along with my sighted peers. As a history student I could take copious notes, writing rapidly with my wonderfully convenient and portable pocket slate and stylus. It was possible to take six pages of notes during a single class, which I could study independently at my own pace as I was preparing for a major test. After Brailling the examination questions, I was free to work on my own, typing the answers for the benefit of my sighted instructors. In a word, because I was Braille literate, I was able to read and write my way to college honors at graduation time.

Because I was fortunate enough to have learned Braille music at the School for the Blind, I was able to memorize works of outstanding classical and romantic composers to play in recital during my junior year in college for audiences of several hundred. I was later to have the opportunity to teach piano to sighted children.

As a teacher of blind children and adults, I could give my knowledge of Braille to others, helping in my turn to foster Braille literacy for them. As a social worker and case worker in New Jersey, I kept Braille records for every one of my clients. From these Braille files I could type continuing records for children in

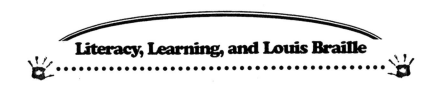

Literacy, Learning, and Louis Braille

foster care, for teenage runaway cases, and for the youngsters known as truants and incorrigibles. In this way I could prepare for court reviews and court hearings at which my recommendations for positive programs were sought as a means of fostering a better quality of life for these troubled young people.

As a mother of three children in a single-parent household, Braille labeling helped me deal with the monthly bills and keep the accounting records of the funds coming in and going out.

When my children were still minors, a growing hearing loss for me caused a termination of regular employment and necessitated seeking work in areas which did not require a keen sense of hearing. A kind friend presented the idea of Braille proofreading. I latched onto this possibility and studied for certification. For many years I served as a proofreader for a private agency producing Braille books and magazines. Currently I work as a part-time proofreader of Braille textbooks for blind children in our schools. To sum up, Braille literacy skills have helped me to achieve fulfillment in every major aspect of my life—as a student; as a teacher; as a case worker; as an employee for a Braille production house; and, above all, as a mother, dedicated to giving a real future to my children. I could not have done it without the ability to read and write Braille.

The Bridge to Braille

Modern technology is fast, functional, advantageous, and handy. Using tapes and speech synthesizers can be an adequate way of obtaining vital information, but listening is not the same as reading, and talking is not the same as writing. The most marvelous and magnificent of all computers, the human brain, is available through the medium of Braille. I thank you, Louis Braille, for providing these six tiny dots—the nucleus from which the whole Braille system has evolved. With these six dots it is possible to retrieve a whole world of education and experience, to understand a lifetime of personal growth and happiness, and to achieve the highest level of independence. With your help and the help of my blind friends I have found opportunities which could not have been attained without you—I have discovered the promise and enjoyed the reality of independence.

Making Whole Language Work
by Carol Castellano

Whole language is an approach to teaching reading and writing which differs in many ways from the traditional system in which most of us learned to read and write. In the traditional approach, children are grouped by reading ability and reading is taught during a certain period each day. Students read from basal readers, the grade by grade reading books which contain words chosen for their "readability" at a certain grade level. Phonics, spelling, and grammar are each taught as separate skills at separate times. The traditional approach might be characterized as "skill-based."

In whole language classrooms a great deal of time during the school day is given over to reading and writing. In place of basal readers, "trade books" are used, authentic works of fiction and nonfiction that can be purchased at a book store. Instead of being grouped according to reading ability, all students read the various trade books. Students are exposed to a wide variety of materials, structures, and styles, and also to the rich, poetic, and often complex language of real literature. Skills such as phonics and spelling are

---

This article first appeared in *Future Reflections*, Vol. 13, No. 3, Fall 1994.

worked on in the context of what the children are reading and writing and are integrated into other curriculum areas. The whole language approach might be called "meaning-" or "content-based."

Other hallmarks of the whole language approach include student choice of reading material and shared and cooperative reading and writing activities, meant to develop appreciation, reflection, thinking, language, and speaking skills. Reading and writing are integrated into all curriculum areas. Teachers encourage intellectual risk-taking instead of rote memorization and answers and subscribe to the idea that the learning is in the doing, thereby placing emphasis on the process of writing and not just on the finished product.

The whole language approach has provoked much discussion and controversy. Proponents of the approach say that it works—children not only learn to read and write with more pleasure and ease, but also become eager, independent, confident, lifelong readers and learners.

Those who object to the trend toward whole language fear that the approach is too loose and leaves too much to chance. The flexibility of whole language is in direct contrast to the controlled nature of traditional programs. Traditional teachers know and rely on the controlled vocabulary and skills checklists of basal readers and workbooks to gauge

Making Whole Language Work

the progress of their students. Some feel it would be chaotic to try to keep track of what the children know and don't know if children read books of their own choosing and if reading is dispersed throughout the day. They fear the loss of formal phonics instruction. Some opponents of whole language are afraid children will not learn how to read. Some simply do not want to change. Despite the controversy, the whole language approach has been adopted in many school districts across the country.

What happens when a Braille student enters a whole language classroom? When my daughter entered first grade, the staff—committed, experienced whole language teachers who had never had a blind student before—expressed great reservations. They believed that she would not be able to participate successfully in the program. One even suggested that she change schools! The teachers expressed many reasons for fearing that whole language would not work with a Braille reader. Due to the need to introduce Braille contractions in advance, they felt Serena would not be able to cope with the random vocabulary found in trade books. A controlled vocabulary as found in basal readers, the teachers reasoned, would make for easier reading for Serena. In addition, they would have no lists of new vocabulary prepared to give to the Braille teacher as they would with basal readers.

The Bridge to Braille

Since trade books would also be used for subjects such as social studies and science, the teachers thought the reading for those subjects, too, would be too complicated. They wondered if it would be possible to get all the necessary books Brailled, since whole language requires many more books than just one textbook for each subject. And lastly, the teachers did not want to give up their freedom to use a wonderful poem or activity they found the night before because they would not have it in Braille the next day for Serena. They also felt that this would limit what would be available to the rest of the children in the class.

When I analyzed what was being said, I realized that the concerns being expressed by experienced whole language teachers about whole language for a Braille student were identical to the concerns expressed by traditional teachers about whole language for any student! The concerns boiled down to one fundamental idea: we really don't know how to do this and make it work!

Serena has been in our school district's whole language program for two-and-a-half years now and as I write this (mid-third grade), she sits contentedly reading a Bobbsey Twins book. I think all her teachers would agree that Serena has fully and successfully participated in the whole language program and that

Making Whole Language Work

she has certainly learned how to read! The inclusion of this Braille student in the program was accomplished without increased burden on the Braille teacher and without restricting the materials the teachers—and other students—could use. Several strategies were employed to make for a successful whole language experience (many of which would apply to any reading program). Here are some of our ideas:

- Much advance planning and preparation was done so that books and materials were ready on time. Books were chosen well in advance (approximately seven months). Teachers were aware of already-Brailled books and books on computer disk which could be quickly obtained in Braille. The teachers took care to let the Braille transcribers know which books and materials would be needed for September and for each subsequent month.
- We acted as a team—classroom teacher, teacher's aide, Braille teacher, and I—to discuss, plan, adapt, trouble-shoot, and problem-solve.
- The Braille teacher previewed books for new contractions and taught them in advance until all contractions had been taught. When Serena did not recognize a contraction in class, the teachers looked it up on a "cheat sheet" and

THE BRIDGE TO BRAILLE

told her what it was. (Incidentally, with trade books, sighted children, too, are challenged with interesting new vocabulary! A blind student can simply participate with the others in whatever vocabulary activities the class is doing.)
- Instead of taking Serena out of class for every lesson, the Braille teacher spent a great deal of time in the classroom, integrating the Braille lesson with the classroom reading activities.
- Reading speed was an issue for the longer passages in "chapter books." At home we practiced speedier-reading exercises and games. We were also advised to have Serena read EVERY NIGHT!
- We taught Serena how to "skim" so that she could follow along efficiently when others were reading aloud.
- The teacher occasionally sent home the book the class would be reading next, for Serena to preview. Sometimes she sent a book home for Serena to finish reading chapters.
- A print copy or photocopy of the book was sent home for all books that Serena was reading, including student-choice and library books. In this way, when Serena got to single-spaced, double-sided Braille books (second grade level and up), anyone, even those not familiar with

Making Whole Language Work

Braille, could follow along as Serena read and provide ordinary help when needed.

- An M-Print, a modified computer printer which translates Braille into print, was attached to the Braille writer so that Serena's writing—daily journals, comprehension questions, reports, paragraphs, etc.—was immediately accessible to her non-Braille reading teachers.
- The school purchased a Braille Blazer (a Braille embosser from Blazie Engineering). Attached to a regular computer, the Blazer enabled the teachers to type in material and produce Braille immediately, thus preserving the teachers' freedom to use newly found materials without excluding their blind student and resulting in access to more Braille for Serena.

I am happy that my daughter was given the opportunity to take part in the school's whole language program and that she is progressing well in it. In addition to reaping what seem to be the benefits of the whole language approach, she has been allowed to experience what everyone else is experiencing. Our conclusion is that with proper planning, teamwork, flexibility, and careful outlay of funds, blind children can successfully participate in a whole language reading program.

A Parent's Guide to the Slate and Stylus
by Barbara Cheadle

If, after reading the title of this article, you have just asked yourself "Isn't the slate and stylus obsolete?" or "Isn't the slate and stylus too hard for children to learn how to use?" or "What is a slate and stylus?" then I hardly need to say more about the need for this guide. For, you see, the answer to the first two questions is a resounding *No!* No, the slate is not obsolete, and no, it is not too difficult for even small children to learn how to use. As for the last question, "What is a slate and stylus?" let me just say that it is the cheapest, simplest, and most portable method for writing Braille. If your mind is still buzzing with questions, and you are not satisfied with the answers I just gave, then I was right. This guide is long overdue! Read on!

Review of the Braille System

Braille was first developed about 1820 by a young Frenchman named Louis Braille. He created Braille by modifying a system of night writing which was intended for use on board ships. He did this work as a very young man and had it complete by the time he was about eighteen. He and his friends at the school

---

Barbara Cheadle is President of the National Organization of Parents of Blind Children and Editor of *Future Reflections.* This article first appeared in *Future Reflections,*Vol. 13, No. 3, Fall 1994.

THE BRIDGE TO BRAILLE

for the blind he attended found that reading and writing dots was much faster than reading raised print letters which could not be written by hand. The development of this system by young Louis Braille is now recognized as the most important single development in making it possible for the blind to get a good education.

It took more than a century, however, before people would accept Braille as an excellent way for the blind to read and write. Even today many people underestimate the effectiveness of Braille. While tapes and records are enjoyable, Braille is essential for note-taking and helpful for studying such things as math, spelling, and foreign languages.

Experienced Braille readers, however, read Braille at speeds comparable to print readers—200 to 400 words per minute. Such Braille readers say that the only limitation of Braille is that there isn't enough material available.

Braille consists of arrangements of dots which make up letters of the alphabet, numbers, and punctuation marks. The basic Braille symbol is called the Braille cell and consists of six dots arranged in the formation of a rectangle, three dots high and two across. Other symbols consist of only some of these six dots. The six dots are commonly referred to by number according to their position in the cell.

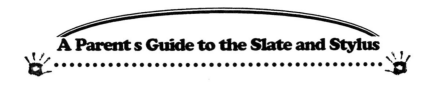
A Parent's Guide to the Slate and Stylus

There are no different symbols for capital letters in Braille. Capitalization is accomplished by placing a dot 6 in the cell just before the letter that is capitalized. The first ten letters of the alphabet are used to make numbers. These are preceded by a number sign which is dots 3-4-5-6. Thus, 1 is number sign *a*; 2 is number sign *b*; 10 is number sign *a-j* and 193 is number sign *a-i-c*.

Braille is written on heavy paper, and the raised dots prevent the pages from lying smoothly together as they would in a print book. Therefore, Braille books are quite bulky. Some abbreviations are used in standard American Braille in order to reduce its bulk. These must be memorized, but most Braille users find them convenient, rather than a problem.

What Is a Slate and Stylus?

A slate and stylus is to a Braille reader what a pen or pencil is to a print reader. Like the pen or pencil the slate and stylus is inexpensive, portable, and simple to use. From taking notes in a classroom to jotting down a phone number, the uses and advantages of the slate to the blind are as many and as varied as those of the pencil or pen are to the sighted.

Just as the pen or pencil is designed to place a visible mark on a piece of paper, the slate and stylus is designed to punch (emboss) raised, tactile bumps or

The Bridge to Braille

dots onto a page. Since Braille is a very exact system –the dots in the Braille cell must be precisely spaced–it wouldn't do to attempt to punch dots freehand onto a page. In order to hand-Braille accurately, there must be a puncher (the **stylus**) which, when pressed into the paper, will raise a tactile Braille dot, and a guide (the **slate**) which will allow the user to punch the dots into precise positions.

Just as pens and pencils come in a variety of styles and sizes, so do slates and styluses. All, however, have common characteristics. The typical stylus is about two inches long. It has a half-inch metal point for punching the dot into the page, and a one-and-a-half-inch wooden handle with a rounded knob at the end so it may be firmly and comfortably gripped by the index finger and thumb. Although the handle may vary on different types of styluses, all will have a metal point for embossing Braille dots.

The typical pocket slate is made either of metal or plastic. It is hinged so that there is a guide under the paper and a guide on top. The slate is about the width of an average piece of paper (8½ inches wide) and four lines of Braille high (a little less than 2 inches). The top piece of the guide has small, evenly spaced openings the precise size and shape of the Braille cell. These are sometimes called *windows*. The bottom guide has small indentations so that the Braille dots

will be consistent in shape and size. Again, slates come in different models to suit different writing needs. There is a slate, for example, especially designed to be used as a guide for 3 x 5 note cards. All slates, however, will have a top and bottom guide as described. Together, the typical slate and stylus weigh about two ounces. Both are easily carried in a pocket or purse.

Why Should Blind Children Learn to Use the Slate and Stylus?

For all the same reasons that sighted children learn to write with a pencil and pen. Think about it. Sighted children have had access to typewriters, tape recorders, and even computers for years. Yet, none of these devices has replaced the need for pencil and pen. The ability to take quick, legible notes with a cheap, simple, portable device is important for both print readers and Braille readers. A slate doesn't use batteries or an electric outlet. It can be carried in a pocket. It is cheap to replace and inexpensive enough that several may be purchased at one time–just like pens. The slate and stylus allows the Braille reader to write down information he or she can immediately read and review anywhere, anytime. A student may easily take a slate and stylus with him or her on school or family trips, to summer camp, Sunday school class, scout meetings–anyplace a pencil can go, a slate and stylus can go. Students can write classroom notes; take a telephone message; take down names, addresses, and telephone numbers; and write out all types of Braille labels and lists with a slate and stylus.

How Does the Slate and Stylus Compare to Other Methods of Writing Braille or Taking Notes?

Most children today begin writing with a Braille writing machine. This may be what your child is currently using. These machines are comparable to typewriters. The Braille writer has a keyboard of only six keys and a space bar, instead of one key for each letter of the alphabet. These keys can be pushed separately or all together. If they are all pushed at the same time they will cause six dots to be raised on the paper in the formation of a Braille cell. Pushing various combinations of the keys on the Braille writer produces different letters of the alphabet and other Braille symbols. The Braille writer is about the size of a medium size typewriter, but is much heavier at ten pounds.

The Braille writer is excellent for writing and editing reports, doing class assignments in the elementary grades, doing math problems, keeping financial records, and generally any Braille writing which does

A Parent's Guide to the Slate and Stylus

not require moving the Braille writer from place to place frequently. The Braille writer's bulk and weight make it a poor choice for most note-taking tasks when students begin moving from class to class in school. It is impossible, of course, to slip a Braille writer into a pocket or purse as one does with a slate and stylus.

Sometimes students believe that a tape recorder will handle all their note-taking needs. Although tape recorders are useful to blind students, they are not good note-taking devices. Note-taking means sifting the information as one listens and making decisions about what is important to write down and what is not. It also means condensing and organizing the information as one writes. It is not possible to do any of this quickly or well with a tape recorder. Besides, students who record an hour lecture must spend another hour listening to it–and even more time studying from it. If they had taken Braille notes in class, they could skim through those notes in less than half the time that it would take to study from a taped lecture.

There is also, of course, a whole array of electronic Braille note-taking devices (such as the Braille 'n Speak), talking computers, and Braille printers for students to choose from today. The Braille note-taking devices are especially popular among high school

THE BRIDGE TO BRAILLE

students, college students, and professionals. It is significant, however, that the most versatile and efficient of these students and professionals are those who also keep a slate handy in their desks or pockets. Even the Director of the International Braille and Technology Center for the Blind–a facility which displays a sample of every Braille and speaking device for the blind in the world–keeps a slate in his suit pocket. For quick, ordinary note-taking needs, the slate still can't be beaten.

How Fast Can a Student Write with a Slate and Stylus?

As fast as a sighted student can write notes with a pen or pencil. However, good instruction and daily practice are as important for the Braille student as they are for the sighted student. If the blind student is not keeping up and complains that the slate is too slow, it is probably due to inadequate instruction and/or practice. One author of a slate and stylus teaching manual suggests that blind students should be able to write a minimum of 15 to 20 words per minute by the time they enter high school. This speed is based upon timed trials in which the student writes out complete sentences with correct spelling and punctuation. Obviously, as the author points out, much faster speed can be obtained when using note-taking shortcuts.

A Parent's Guide to the Slate and Stylus

One blind woman worked several years as a note-taker with a state agency which investigated equal employment opportunity complaints. The job required taking notes at formal hearings. Some hearings were recorded, but note-takers were needed for those who objected to this. The notes did not need to be verbatim, but they did need to be thorough and accurate. Some hearings lasted as long as three hours. She could not use a Braille writer for it was deemed too loud and intrusive by the hearing judges. So, she used a slate and stylus to take the notes and typed them up later to turn in. She soon developed a reputation for being an outstanding note-taker, and hearing judges frequently requested her services. The woman learned to write with the slate in first grade, when she was six years old.

How Long Does It Take to Learn to Use the Slate and Stylus?

How long does it take to learn to use a pen or pencil? This depends. It takes only seconds to learn how to hold the pencil and make a mark on a piece of paper. It takes a little longer to learn how to hold the pencil correctly when writing words and letters, and of course it takes much longer to learn how to print and write cursive correctly and legibly. It partly takes a good deal of time because the student

THE BRIDGE TO BRAILLE

is learning the letters while he or she is simultaneously learning to write them.

The same is true when learning to write Braille with the slate and stylus. The rudiments of using the slate and stylus can be learned in minutes. Proficiency in using the slate comes with months or years of regular practice and usage (as in the case of very young children). Remember, this is also true for sighted students learning to write with a pencil.

As a parent you may be wondering how fast you could learn to use the slate and stylus. The National Organization of Parents of Blind Children sponsors Beginning Braille for Parents workshops. In three hours parents learn the basics of reading Braille and writing it with the slate and stylus. They learn how to insert the paper into the slate frame, how to correctly hold the stylus while punching the dots onto the paper, how to use their fingers to guide the stylus and keep their place, and how to move the slate guide down the paper as needed. Then, as they learn Braille letters, they learn how to use the slate guide to punch in the correct dot positions for the desired letter. Parents leave the workshop feeling that Braille reading and writing is fun and easy! Many continue to study and practice Braille reading and writing on their own.

Of course not everyone can attend a workshop, so at the end of this guide is a list of manuals and other

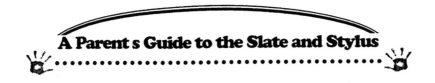

materials which can be used for independent home study of Braille and the slate and stylus.

Are There Any Differences between Learning to Use a Pen or Pencil and Learning to Use a Slate and Stylus?

Yes, but let's first review how they are NOT different: Both systems, as discussed in the questions above, have the same function and advantages and get the job done equally well; both systems take about the same time to learn; and neither system is inherently any more difficult to learn than the other. Please keep these similarities in mind. In the long haul they are more important than the differences.

The differences between the methods of writing arise naturally out of the fact that one is a visual system and one is a tactile system. For example, most people learn to hold a pencil at a slant. But different hand and finger positions and motions are required for slate and stylus usage. For ease and efficiency in punching Braille dots, the stylus must be held in a straight up and down position. Also, punching dots onto a page requires slightly more force than is needed when writing with a pen or pencil. Teachers of blind children often encourage young blind children to play with pop-together toys because this activity develops strength and dexterity in the fingers. This

The Bridge to Braille

dexterity is also required when opening the four-line pocket slate and repositioning the paper.

On the other hand, while sighted students must essentially learn four different ways of forming each letter of the alphabet–print upper-case, print lower-case, cursive upper-case, and cursive lower-case –blind children need to learn only one form for each letter. (As noted in the review of the Braille system at the beginning of this guide, a Braille word is capitalized by simply placing the Braille dot 6 before the letter to be capitalized. This is much simpler to learn than an entire new form for each letter.)

Finally, a person writing Braille with the slate and stylus begins at the right side of the paper and ends the line on the left, since the dots are being produced on the underside of the paper. Of course, the Braille reader reads from left to right, for the dots are then on the top side of the paper. Although this may seem a bit confusing, it need not be at all troublesome, since both reading and writing progress through words and sentences from beginning to end in the same manner.

If a blind student is confused and refers to writing with a slate as "writing backwards," then incorrect teaching methods are likely being used. No respectable elementary teacher in the country, for example, would teach sighted students that a *d* is a

A Parent's Guide to the Slate and Stylus

backward *b*. Of course it is reversed, and of course students figure that out, and of course some students have a few problems because of it. However, correct teaching methods combined with lots of practice solve this difficulty. The same is true of learning to write with a slate and stylus.

When Should Blind Children Learn to Use a Slate and Stylus?

Blind people who started school anytime up to the late fifties or early sixties find this question amusing. Although the first mechanical Braille writing device was invented in 1850, Braille writers were not commonly available to blind students of all ages until after 1951–the year the modern Perkins Brailler went into production. In those early years Braille writing machines–if they were available at all–were used only by students in the higher grades, and one machine was shared by several students. So, what did blind first-graders use all those years before the Braille writer was invented or available to them? Why, the slate and stylus, of course! (This is still true, by the way, in developing nations where Braille writers are far too expensive for common usage.)

Some parents today are successfully experimenting in using the slate and stylus with their blind preschoolers. The children use the slate and stylus for the

THE BRIDGE TO BRAILLE

same purpose that sighted preschoolers use a pencil or other marker: to scribble. Just like a sighted child, a blind child may pretend that his or her scribbles–the Braille dots–are words or even pictures. This gives the child a positive experience with the slate and stylus so that when formal instruction begins he or she is comfortable with the slate and eager to learn to write real words with it.

Today, teaching manuals commonly recommend that the slate and stylus be introduced in the third grade. The author of one manual suggests that students do not need to begin formal instruction with the slate and stylus until entrance into middle school (sixth grade). Students should certainly begin no later than this.

As you can see, there is no consensus on the best time to begin writing instruction with a slate. It can be successfully taught at any time from kindergarten on up. Remember, however, that it is easier to gain the interest and cooperation of younger students. Also, slate and stylus skills should be firmly in place by the time the child is old enough to want and need a truly portable system of writing. If those skills are not in place, the child begins to be subtly excluded from certain activities.

Consider, for example, a typical meeting of a Girl Scout troop of girls grades 3 through 6. The

troop is planning a camp-out. Each patrol within the troop is told to plan a menu for one of the meals, make a grocery list, and take the list to the store to buy the foods. They must also plan one activity–a skit, a game, etc.–for the camp-out. Before they begin planning, however, each patrol must choose one of the girls to be the patrol secretary to keep all necessary notes and lists. Slate and stylus skills would put a blind scout on an equal footing with her sister scouts in handling this necessary task for the group. She would also get early experience with one of the most common jobs in our society. Secretaries are needed everywhere–in business and in volunteer community organizations.

What Is the Best Method for Teaching the Slate and Stylus?

Although there are a few variations in approaches to teaching the slate and stylus, all good teaching manuals adhere to the same basic principles. For example, all the best manuals insist that the word backward never be used when describing or teaching the slate and stylus method of writing. Instead, the authors of these manuals encourage phrases such as *starting side* or *approach side; first column, second column; first side, second side; direction of travel;* and so forth. This approach is essential for the best success.

THE BRIDGE TO BRAILLE

Beyond this, a good teaching manual or method description should provide the following: (1) an explanation of the importance of building motivation and enthusiasm in the student through discussions and demonstrations of the usefulness of the slate and stylus; (2) a thorough description of the sequential steps to take in teaching the student how to physically manipulate the slate and stylus–i.e., inserting paper, holding the stylus, moving the paper down, locating the Braille cell window with the tip of the stylus, and so forth; (3) lesson plans or a sequential list of letters and words to be introduced to the student; (4) miscellaneous information about materials, equipment, and teaching aids; and (5) guidance and suggestions about promoting daily practice and use of the slate and stylus among students.

Listed below are some teaching manuals which meet these criteria. A few of these manuals were written primarily for teachers of newly blind adults. They have been included because parents might find them useful as self-teaching guides and because some of the methods and teaching aids they promote apply to children, too. Also included in this list are manuals or handbooks which include slate and stylus teaching instructions as a chapter or segment of that book. Page and/or chapter numbers are given with these listings.

Teaching the Braille Slate and Stylus
by Philip Mangold
Exceptional Teaching Aids
20102 Woodbine Avenue
Castro Valley, CA 94546
(510) 582-4859 or 1-800-549-6999
www.exceptionalteaching.com

*Teachers' Guide for the McDuffy Reader:
A Braille Primer for Adults*
by Sharon L. M. Duffy
("Teaching Slate Writing," pp. 9-13)
National Federation of the Blind
1800 Johnson Street
Baltimore, MD 21230
(410) 659-9314
www.nfb.org

Braille Writing Simplified
by Claudell Stocker
National Organization of Parents of Blind Children,
A Division of the National Federation of the Blind
1800 Johnson Street
Baltimore, MD 21230
(410) 659-9314
www.nfb.org

THE BRIDGE TO BRAILLE

Slate and Stylus Program from
*PATTERNS: THE PRIMARY BRAILLE SPELLING
AND ENGLISH PROGRAM*, LEVEL C
Hilda Caton, Director
Betty Modaressi, Editor
AMERICAN PRINTING HOUSE FOR THE BLIND
1839 FRANKFORT AVENUE
P.O. BOX 6085
LOUISVILLE, KY 40206-0085
(502) 895-2405 OR 1-800-223-1839
www.aph.org

*HANDBOOK FOR ITINERANT AND RESOURCE TEACHERS
OF BLIND AND VISUALLY IMPAIRED STUDENTS*
by Doris M. Willoughby and Sharon L. M. Duffy
("A Braillewriter in My Pocket," Chapter 18, p. 135)
NATIONAL FEDERATION OF THE BLIND
1800 JOHNSON STREET
BALTIMORE, MD 21230
(410) 659-9314
www.nfb.org

What Kinds of Slates and Styluses Are Available, How Much Do They Cost, and Who Sells Them?

The typical pocket slate and stylus was described under the heading "What is a Slate and Stylus?" The pocket slate, as you will recall, can come either in plastic or metal. The plastic slates are the least

A Parent's Guide to the Slate and Stylus

expensive ($3.00, including the stylus), but are only available in the four-line, 28-cell-per-line size. They are also not as durable as the metal slates.

Metal slates are more expensive but are also available in a wide variety of sizes and styles to meet different needs. Some of these are note-card size slates (six line, 19-cell), with or without a hinge; pocket slates (four line, 27-cell) with a notch for holding labeling tape; one line, 25-cell slates for labeling tape only; pocket slates with an open back so that the Braille can be read without removing the paper from the slate; slates designed exclusively for embossing cassette labels or playing cards; and board or desk slates. Prices vary among sources, of course, but will typically range from $8.00 or $10.00 for the single-line slate to $14.00 to $30.00 for the regular or specialty metal slates and up to $40.00 plus for desk or board slates.

The board slate, which is especially useful to Braille transcribers, comes in three pieces: a sturdy page-size writing surface (much like a clip-board) made of wood, plastic, or masonite board; a heavy-duty metal four-line, 41- or 27-cell slate; and a regular stylus. The board has a clip at the top to hold the Braille paper in place and matching holes down the right and left sides of the board. The slate is like a regular pocket slate with the addition of two small round pegs on the back side of the frame. These pegs,

The Bridge to Braille

when inserted into the matching holes on the sides of the board, hold the slate firmly in place. When the student has completed four lines of Braille the slate is eased out of the holes and slid down to the next set of holes and so on until the page is full.

In addition to the regular stylus described earlier, there are styluses with a flat-sided handle to prevent rolling; pencil shaped styluses; and reversible metal styluses (flat or regular handles) in which the point may be removed and reversed for storage inside the handle. These vary in price from roughly $1.00 to $8.00.

Wooden or metal Braille erasers which flatten unwanted Braille dots are usually available in a price range from $1.00 to $3.00.

Some sources for slates and styluses are:

National Federation of the Blind
Materials Center
1800 Johnson Street
Baltimore, MD 21230
(410) 659-9314
www.nfb.org

AMERICAN PRINTING HOUSE FOR THE BLIND
1839 FRANKFORT AVENUE
P.O. BOX 6085
LOUISVILLE, KY 40206-0085
(502) 895-2405 OR 1-800-223-1839
www.aph.org

HOWE PRESS
175 NORTH BEACON STREET
WATERTOWN, MA 02472
(617) 924-3490
www.perkins/pvt.k12.ma.us

LS&S GROUP
P.O. BOX 673
NORTHBROOK, IL 60065
1-800-468-4789
www.lssgroup.com

About the Authors

Carol Castellano is the parent of a Braille reader. She is President and co-founder of Parents of Blind Children-New Jersey (POBC-NJ), an affiliate of the National Organization of Parents of Blind Children (NOPBC). She received her degree in English literature from Douglass College, Rutgers University, and writes frequently on the education and development of blind children. Carol lives in Madison, NJ, with her husband, Bill Cucco, and their children, Serena and John.

Dawn Kosman is a certified Teacher of the Blind. She received her degree from Dominican College of Blauvelt, New York. She has taught Braille in programs for blind children in New Jersey and New York since 1982. Dawn lives in Effort, PA, with her husband, Kevin, and daughter, Kailee.